To all my dear friends
at the Herald Dept. (and beyond),

You have been part of so many quiet
answers for me — helping with translation
and the new ads for the German and
Spanish Herald, a ... I hope
you may all find some quiet ...
in this book — or at least some
smiles + deep thoughts.

So many thanks to Ricardo, Ana Paula,
Patricia and Maike plus anyone else
involved. I feel such a kinship with
all you are doing—for my goal + motto's
" as the waters cover the sea." God loves
you + so do I, Avril
January 2004

Other Works by the Same Author

Books
      Numberland
      Bird

Musical plays
      Numberland
      Musicland

Music and dialogue recordings
      Numberland
      Numberland Music
      Musicland
      Children's Musicland
      Something Bright and Beautiful
      Bird
      Lessons from Bird

A spiritual journey home

Quiet

Answers

Auriel Wyndham Livezey

MOUNTAINTOP
PUBLISHING

Illustrated by Hank Richter

Cover artwork by Bill Kuhre

Printed in the United States of America
ISBN 1-893930-03-3

Mountaintop Publishing
P.O. Box 15316
Long Beach, CA 90815
(562) 431-0707, fax (562) 598-3308
www.MountaintopPublishing.com

CONTENTS

Introduction

Part One

Part Two

INTRODUCTION

We all like answers spelled out clearly; something we can't miss and don't have to think about twice. Skywriting would be quite acceptable, or perhaps a banner—preferably with our name attached so we know it's for us. "Mary Lou, do not marry that guy from Montreal, be a tour director instead." "Joe, take the job in Washington, but pack lightly." Wouldn't that be nice! However, usually the quiet answer comes without fanfare.

This book will deal with different aspects of both questions and answers. Poetry may even spill out occasionally and hopefully we'll have a few laughs along the way. While learning life lessons may be a serious undertaking, it certainly does not need to be a formal, "black tie" event.

Speaking of formal events, lines of distinction between dress-up and casual wear used to be sharply drawn, just as the written word—particularly on topics of some depth—differed distinctly from everyday speech. However, even as dress has become casual so has writing. Gone is my hat with the flowing chiffon trailing behind it along with my colored gloves, and gone is the more formal approach to writing. The trend today seems to be to write as one speaks.

Now, I must begin with an admission that due to an early classical training this is not something which comes easily, especially when writing about matters of some consequence. Perhaps I should quote a great statesman, I think it was Churchill, as he humorously demonstrated the effect of trying too hard not to end a sentence with a preposition. This new tendency against literary loveliness is something "Up with which I will not put," or at least, it is something up with which I will not easily put.

So I am going to ask for your forbearance and forgiveness in advance should I commit any crime against casualness. And I promise to comb through this manuscript carefully hoping to avoid the formality but, should it creep in, perhaps you could laugh it off with a comment such as, "Oh, there she is at the computer with her large, elegant hat and high heels." That would be very kind of you and would let me off in the process because, you see, I'm not writing for writing's sake but out of great love for the subject.

Conventional wisdom dictates that we should write about what we know best and so in following this advice I'll include only known experiences—my own, and those of family or friends. Most of them are modest experiences proving that quiet answers are readily available for even the small details of our lives and not reserved for only the "big questions." Though the answers have come with a price tag, a lesson that is learned, the cost has always been within reach. And whether it was an executive who felt he had to tell "white lies" or a young mother having to write a sonnet for a college class, I think you will find these examples all point to that source of quiet answers—the unvarying Principle or divine Love that many refer to as the Holy Spirit, the Supreme Being. My own pathway of finding and understanding these answers, and the help I've had, will be included as we go along.

So now I invite you to join me on a little excursion, a spiritual journey into the land of quiet answers.

Part One

Quiet Answers . . . Here and Now

A man, who was stationed with an international organization in Paris and whose daily language was English, was walking down a Parisian street, praying about his future. What was his next step? Where should he go? Turning a corner, he suddenly came face to face with a poster in the window of a travel agency. In large letters and in English it announced, "Go to Britain!" As it turned out, the man did later go to Britain and it was the next right step for him. But no one else heard the question, let alone the answer. To the casual observer, the man was simply pausing in front of a travel advertisement.

Why do answers exist?

Quiet answers do exist. They are always present under any condition, in any place, and are available at any time. They are accessible to each and every one of us regardless of our background, our education, religion, age, gender, socioeconomic status or state of health. As natural as the air we breathe—as constant as the sun that shines—is the answer we need. Our worthiness in no way causes the answer to exist and our unworthiness cannot make it disappear. The answer is not dependent on us—on what we say, think or do—anymore than an answer to a mathematical question would depend on us or vary according to our thinking or actions.

The solution to a mathematical problem is always available since the principle of mathematics is fixed and permanent. In the same way our life questions do have answers because there is a fixed and true Principle of life to which we can turn. This Principle doesn't vary, doesn't play guessing games with us or

13

trifle with our feelings. Infinitely more loving than we can imagine, far surpassing any earthly power and more gentle than the kindest human parent is our heavenly Parent.

What I just took two paragraphs to explain in part, James the Apostle accomplished completely in just one short sentence in which he speaks of gifts, goodness, perfection and illumination while implying that our Parent is an unvarying, heavenly, perfect Principle. "Every good gift and every perfect gift is from above, and cometh down from the Father of lights, with whom is no variableness, neither shadow of turning" (James 1:17). But, of course, James had great teaching.

Is faith going to play a part?

I'm going to be drawing on that teaching for this book because the Book of Books, the Bible, contains insights and wisdom that are just as applicable to today's world as when they were first lived, loved and written down. In other words, they are timeless truths.

Now a reader, fearing a religious skirmish of some kind, may ask at this point if it's necessary to have faith. It can be replied that everyone has faith in one direction or another. We have faith our car will start in the morning (unless you have a chronic complainer for a car) and we have faith the lights will come on when we flick a switch (no reference will be made to California's 2002 energy crunch). Yes, our daily existence is full of faith and we will unashamedly admit it, except when it comes to one area, that of the divine, and then perhaps the need to justify appears.

However, faith in God can only savor of the mystical or mysterious if one doesn't understand God. Of course, that "mystery" element is true of most anything, such as an appliance we use or an airplane we fly, if we don't understand it. I've read accounts of aboriginal people, who had never before seen a plane or a pilot, believing they had been visited by a deity from above. That might have made the pilot either extremely happy or extremely nervous depending on the religious rituals involved. Also along these "mysterious" lines, there was the wonderfully insightful and humorous tale about a Coke™ bottle dropping from the sky in the film "The Gods Must be Crazy."

The enigma of the bottle dropping from the sky is not unlike some of our own queries about life. Why do certain experiences just appear in our lives? How come that wonderful job just dropped into someone's lap? When it comes down to it, we really don't love a mystery, at least, not an unsolvable one.

This is all to say that in our modern, pragmatic world faith in the understandable is allowable, so that is exactly what this book hopes to do—explore the understandable realm of quiet answers.

Understanding the spiritual dimension.

The man who made a dramatic transition from faithless to faithful—from Saul to Paul—wrote to the Hebrews about the part that faith plays in gaining access to solutions: " . . . he that cometh to God must believe that he is, and that he is a rewarder of them that diligently seek him" (Hebrews 11:6). But Paul was not making a pitch for blind faith without understanding, he was only referencing a starting point. It was as though he had said to a child, "Now you have to believe there is a principle of mathematics we can go to for our math questions, because that's where you'll find the answer to the problems in your arithmetic book."

Yes, that was a beginning. But Paul didn't leave it there, at the level of faith, but went on to explain the nature of our divine Principle in understandable language to the men of Athens whom he addressed while standing on Mars Hill. Paul didn't like what he had seen; ". . . I perceive that in all things ye are too superstitious. For as I passed by, and beheld your devotions, I found an altar with this inscription, TO THE UNKNOWN GOD. Whom therefore ye ignorantly worship, him declare I unto you" (Acts 17:22,23). Then he did just that. He explained that God is the creator of all, that there is a universal brotherhood, and that we can't worship what is spiritual by material means. But when he came to the part about resurrection from the dead that was too much for his audience—strong believers in death that they must have been—and some began to mock him. So he left.

If we can agree that there is a divine source for answers, then we have the starting point that Paul indicates. Of course, even if you choose not to agree that would not invalidate the source or even the answers that I'm going to be sharing with you in this book. So, if you are of that persuasion perhaps you might still enjoy these accounts and (as they say in the theater) suspend your disbelief for awhile and follow the play as it unfolds before you. You can always make up your mind at the end as you would after a television show of "true" or "false" stories—remembering, of course, that truth is often stranger than fiction.

I'd like to bring mathematics back into the equation on the basis that we do have a divine source for our answers. Taking our desires to God, the Principle of our lives, is like taking our math questions to the principle of mathematics. It's the most intelligent thing we can do. We find that mathematics and true spirituality share in common the element of faith. This is just one of many points of convergence. We believe in and trust the source, the mathematical principle in one case and the divine Principle in the other, to have the answers we need—and we make our approach with this faith. And the more we understand the principle of math and the more we understand our divine Principle, God, the more our faith increases in both.

In thinking of the Holy Spirit we may recall that Christ Jesus used the term Spirit when speaking of God and he explained the nature of God as that of a loving Parent. He even told us that, " . . . your Father knoweth what things ye have need of, before ye ask him" (Matthew 6:8).

Now it must logically follow that all the good things which God, who is Spirit, has provided for us are spiritual. So how does all that spirituality translate to the human scene, which certainly seems limited and overflowing with material things? Might not that spiritual good come to us in the same way that chalk on a blackboard represents the invisible principle of mathematics? Might it not come to us in useful symbols, not as numbers but as food, clothing, a job, companionship? Yes, spiritual good will cover all our human needs, but not necessarily all our human wants.

On the journey home.

After settling the faith issue, other questions might appear. What if we find ourselves right in the middle of a situation we know to be wrong? How do we get out of it and do we have the right to be rewarded as Paul promised? Have you ever felt you didn't deserve a good answer so you didn't expect to hear one? But again, the answer does not depend on you or me. Oh, the listening part may depend on us but not the answer. It's not because of our goodness; it's due to God's goodness, that the answer exists. It is because of His nature that the quiet answer is waiting for us. In fact, it is there before we ask the question or know that we have a need.

Our Principle of life is God and God is Love and Love simply loves. End of report! Now, if a kind human parent allows for a turnaround, how much more is divine Love waiting forever to love and bless us. That was the message of Jesus' parable about the prodigal son who, after wasting his inheritance, came to his senses and returned home to what might almost be described as a hero's welcome.

Some of the sweetest words in our language and the most touching are, "I'm going home." Didn't we feel a pull at our heartstrings as the little film creature E.T. pointed his bony finger to the sky with the wish to "phone home." And how we empathized as he stood in the forest looking upward repeating the one word, "home, home."

When my family traveled and lived in many countries, I remember thinking now and then that I wanted to go home but I never could put my finger, bony or otherwise, on that exact spot. I remember reviewing the countries mentally, where I came from and where I'd lived, and though a couple of them definitely called to me, somehow I knew that my yearning was not for a physical location. It was not to be found in geography. I came to the conclusion that the yearning to go home simply meant being closer to God, going home spiritually by doing what was right, becoming more conscious of goodness, purity, peace and love. Though it's been many years since then, I feel that teenage conclusion is still a good answer to the heart's desire for home.

We are all on a spiritual journey, whether we know it or not, just as we are all riding on the outside of a spacecraft hurtling through the universe and around the sun at quite a speed even while sitting quietly (perhaps oblivious to this fact) in a chair at home.

Not everyone has had a loving childhood but many do know the warmth of belonging and the feeling of being physically at home. However, even the humanly-satisfied heart can yearn for a deeper contentment—the wonderful joy of feeling spiritually at home. I wonder how many people are actually heavenly homesick and don't know it. Have you ever felt an unnamed longing? Or, on the other hand, have you ever experienced a special feeling of peace and contentment that envelops you without any external reason attached to it? Even without a direct mental effort attached to it? I've felt that on a few occasions, perhaps when only sitting in a car waiting for someone. To me, that is the feeling of going home.

The Joni Mitchell song "Both Sides Now" ends with the plaintive words, "It's life's illusions I recall. I really don't know life at all." We are all being called to go home, to leave life's illusions, not through suffering and definitely not through death, but through the understanding of what divine Life, God, truly is. No one is left out. Divine Love has no favorites. In his Sermon on the Mount, Christ Jesus described just how impartial our heavenly Father is: " . . . he maketh his sun to rise on the evil and on the good, and sendeth rain on the just and on the unjust" (Matthew 5:45). No partiality in this Parent! All have the ability to turn to this perfect Principle of life.

But even some of the best and most golden characters on our human scene might admit they don't know what it is to be at one with God, to be spiritually at home. There seems to be a human estrangement from the divine.

Part of that separated sense may have to do with the fact that humans can't understand why God lets bad things happen, especially to good people. But blaming our divine Principle for human errors makes just about as much sense as blaming the principle of mathematics for the mistakes we find in our checkbooks. We only need to enter the errorless world of mathematics in order to reconcile that bank balance. Likewise, we need to understandingly enter the errorless dimension of Spirit, in order to find complete harmony. The Supreme Being no more causes or allows human errors than does the unvarying principle of mathematics.

This is the reconciliation the Bible speaks of—the necessity for the human experience to become reconciled to the divine facts. Then it is patently obvious that divinity never knew of, nor allowed, such errors as sin, disease or death.

The human belief that one can be estranged from the source of all that is good and spiritual, estranged from Life, our divine Principle, is impossible—as ridiculous as assuming that a number can be estranged from the principle of mathematics. The human illusions about life—"life's illusions"—need to be dispelled. Eternal Life doesn't need changing, only our concept of it does. As the clouds of human errors fade away, we'll see the unity with God, the good, the perfection, joy, spiritual life and immortality that have been here all along. The dispelling of these clouds is our spiritual journey home.

Divine Love is not only waiting for us at home but is with us every step of the way, lighting our pathway with quiet answers. So, whether we are making a total mess of our lives or doing reasonably well, this perfect Principle has road maps ready and available for each one of us. Yes, there are road maps designed for our spiritual journey and we will find, if we pay close attention, that they are very well marked indeed.

U-Turns Are Always Allowed

Everyday decisions do have an impact on our human goals and they certainly do on our spiritual goals. The friends we choose, the line of work, a marriage all will either hinder or help us on our way. Life is not a static event. It's a progression. So it's important to choose activities and life-traveling companions with a journey in mind. U-turns may sometimes be necessary but they are not all equal. It helps to take regular stock of our lives and ask questions. Am I making bad decisions while basically on the right road and, if so, why? Or am I on the wrong road, going in the wrong direction, altogether? Let's consider the following examples.

Just a mistake.

A young woman accepted a proposal of marriage and moved to another city where her fiancé lived. This meant leaving a job she liked and had worked at quite successfully for a year and a half. As weeks and even months went by, she became increasingly unsure about her marriage plans and the move itself. When she prayed about the situation there was no clear message given her to stay. In fact, what appeared to be a chance encounter on the street and a brief conversation with a stranger pointed her in the opposite direction.

As the stranger talked about her own life, the details so paralleled events that were going on in the young woman's family that she realized it was necessary for her to leave for a couple of reasons. She needed to leave because of her uncertainty about the marriage and also for her family.

So she moved back to her former area and then broke off the engagement. Her decision was not an easy one but, because it came through prayer, she obeyed. Now it appeared she'd have to begin all over again in the job market, go back to square one. As she prepared to do this, she earnestly prayed, "Dear God, please erase my mistake."

While visiting friends at her previous place of employment she found her position had not been filled in the five months that she had been absent. Moreover it turned out that the management would like to have her back just as much as she wanted to return. However there was one problem: Due to fact this was a state organization, if the position were to be filled again it would need to be opened up to other applicants, and this would involve time and effort. The problem appeared to have no easy solution. The young woman continued to pray for guidance, acknowledging that God would place her where she needed to be.

After carefully considering the situation, the management developed an unexpected option that satisfied everyone involved and met all the requirements. They simply rescinded the young woman's resignation. Her mistake was totally erased. It was as if she had never resigned. Interestingly, when praying about this, the young woman had pledged her willingness to accept the same pay or less just to have the position back again. However, as she resumed work she was actually given a small raise and her progress continued in that organization with increasing responsibility and remuneration to match.

Here were the important points of that young woman's prayer: She knew there was a source for answers so she asked for guidance; she knew God is Love and has only good for His children; she listened and waited for guidance and, when she heard it, she had the willingness and courage to obey. These fundamentals—the willingness to turn to God, understanding God, praying, listening and obeying—return over and over again and are basic to solving life problems as we journey on.

What about the question?

Now another point seems so apparent as not needing to be mentioned, but I'll mention it anyway. A former neighbor of mine, a member of an Eastern Orthodox church, called me from across the country and asked why she wasn't getting any answers about employment. (This woman and I had discussed God's goodness and guidance on a number of occasions.)

She described the church service she had attended and how during that short service she had praised God and affirmed his goodness but hadn't received answers. I inquired, "Did you ask God any questions? Did you ask for divine guidance or for wisdom?" After all, James had said, " . . . ye have not, because ye ask not" (James 4:2). Then came a distinct pause followed by the admission that she hadn't asked anything at all. I mentioned that it is very difficult to get an answer if you haven't asked a question. She laughed with relief and decided she had better talk with God again.

Exactly who wanted what?

A seemingly brilliant idea we come up with just might be someone else's desire that we mistake for our own. If we allow ourselves to be wrongly influenced then we can count on having to backtrack. Perhaps this explains what happened when a family took in a teenager from another country at the request of a third party. It was only going to be for a couple of weeks as the teenager's plans to stay with another family had fallen through.

The visit was going quite well and the young mother enjoyed conversations with the teenager. Suddenly, in the midst of one of these, and for no explicable reason, she had an overwhelming desire to invite the girl to stay longer, even for a year or so. The teenager could go to school and help her with the children. It looked like a plus in all directions. The woman quickly blurted out her invitation (which was immediately accepted) without even consulting her husband and other family members. This looked like a problem in the making, especially when the parents of the girl also gave their ready agreement.

The situation appeared even more complicated when it became obvious that the teenager was accustomed to a rather easy lifestyle with rules that were far more flexible in her own home than in her host home. Deeply disappointed at her lack of wisdom, the woman realized she had been mentally influenced into an action that she didn't want to take and one that she never would have taken had she thought it over. She had mentally heard the girl's desire to stay longer and accepted it as her own idea. With remorse and some anxiety she prayed about the solution.

The way out, the U-turn, was not an easy road. It was hardly a few days later that the woman's husband lost his job and was out of full-time employment for over a year. At least the offer could be retracted with the complete understanding of the teenager and her family. What a price to pay for being unduly influenced! Oh, I suppose we could think the man might have lost his job anyway and that it had nothing to do with the unwise action. Hard to say! I do know that the woman felt the two occurrences were linked and that losing the job, as difficult as it was, might actually have been the lesser of the two problems.

Yes, some lessons do cost more than others. The little family made it through that period and God's love for them was proved many times over. This experience certainly points up the need to be very sure of what or who is pushing us where. God's will is wise, impartial and blesses everyone but human will is unwise and selective for its own ends and purposes. Some signs of mental influence are: a rush to do something without thinking it through; unwillingness to talk it over with others involved; unwillingness to pray about a decision; a mental haze or mental sleepiness. The influence might come from another person, or it might be mass media, or advertising that takes over our thinking.

However, it could also be our own unresolved character traits like wilfulness or impetuosity that push us into a wrong decision. Whether it's our own impetuosity, our own wilfulness or another's, the spiritual journey won't allow for it. Peter's impetuous rush to join Jesus walking on the water almost ended in submerging him. Suddenly afraid because he was out of his spiritual depth, Peter began to sink and Jesus had to take his hand in order to save him. "Impetuosity Incline" or "Wilfulness Way" are not on our spiritual road map and we'll have to redo that phase of the journey if we rush headlong down those detours.

How many times?

Now, the young woman who had left her job and the mother issuing unwise invitations were endeavoring to travel in a right direction. They were just making bad decisions along the way, decisions that could affect their spiritual path and slow them down. We might call these the minor U-turns. How many times are we allowed to backtrack and adjust our course? As many times as necessary.

Then there's the major type of U-turn such as Paul made. He wasn't merely making bad decisions on the right road but was totally in the wrong direction. By persecuting others, he was traveling far away from home. He was being wrongly influenced "big time," as the saying goes, and not necessarily by people alone but by the unseen influences of hate and prejudice. You could say he was taking the wrong subjects in this earthly school; that is, until he came to a grinding halt. Paul's total turnabout, his new direction, had a worldwide and timeless effect on others' lives.

A total change of direction obviously requires a total change of mind. Paul had turned away from hate and prejudice towards love and a burning desire to serve mankind. Having come from that background, it's not difficult to understand why Paul was often strong in his language and why he urged the Philippians (2:5) to follow the perfect example of being influenced rightly; "Let this mind be in you, which was also in Christ Jesus."

Christ Jesus was able to maintain his spiritual standpoint and the spiritual goal of showing us the way home, the path to spiritual reality. In the process he had to resist many temptations: " . . . in all points tempted like as we are, yet without sin" (Hebrews 4:15) was the description Paul gave of Jesus. And Matthew, the disciple, relates how Jesus refused temptations though offered great rewards if he would bow down to the material world and worship it instead of God, who is Spirit. Jesus consistently refused to be influenced to take a minor or major detour and steadily maintained his course.

Of the many wonderful examples Jesus gave along the way, one of the most incredibly kind has to be the example and teaching of forgiveness. No more was it to be an "eye-for-an-eye" vigilante type of justice. When Peter asked him how many times he should forgive his brother who sinned against him, suggesting seven times, Jesus replied, "I say not unto thee, Until seven times: but, Until seventy times seven" (Matthew 18:22). He then went on to explain, through a parable, that if we don't understand the concept of forgiveness enough to forgive another then we won't be able to receive forgiveness ourselves. Obviously, if we won't allow someone else the privilege of a U-turn, we will be less likely to believe one is possible for us.

70 X 7 = as many times as needed!

Let's for a moment take out the human argument of who deserves what, and think of it in more infinite and impersonal terms, because that really helps. Is there ever a time when we can't correctly employ the principle of mathematics? Can we make mistakes for too many years so that the principle of math will finally say to us, "You've had it! I've given you all these chances to use the multiplication table and you've messed up every time, so now it's not available to you anymore." Hardly! The principle remains to be understood and conformed to and we have an infinite number of opportunities to do just that.

Jesus obviously had that concept of our heavenly Principle, divine Love. It makes perfect sense when we think about it, if we can leave hurt feelings, personal reaction or societal retribution out of the equation. This means that anyone, anytime can make a major U-turn, as the man in the next story found out.

A U-turn that helped so many.

A young man literally went into his closet to pray because he was part of a noisy family and this was the only quiet spot he could find. How he came to be there in the first place is a story in itself. Part of a hard-drinking crowd in an advertising agency, he found his life going down a questionable road. There was quite a turnabout needed and, when it came, it took his whole life in a completely unexpected direction. His acquaintances changed, his body changed, his profession changed and he later found himself giving lectures internationally on the subject of spiritual healing.

Here was a man (called Glen) who had felt uncomfortable about giving talks to more than five people at a time, now speaking to a crowd of five thousand in New York's Central Park. Though two thousand of them were walking and eating while he spoke, he never lost track of what he was saying. He stayed on course.

How did this transformation come about? I'll use excerpts from his second lecture—"Who Do You Think You Are?"—to piece it together for you. His lecture began with the biblical story of Jacob, who had deceived his father, with his mother's help, and robbed his brother of the inheritance. After recounting Jacob's struggle to be made anew, Glen tells of his own struggles. Here is what he said:

> Take the experience of a man I know. He was in advertising. His career was blossoming. He had regular raises in pay and improvements in title and responsibility. He prided himself on being able to get along with clients.
>
> Yet from time to time he'd had some anxious moments. Sometimes when he'd been caught by a client in a story of why this or that wasn't done, with sweating hands and brow he'd cover up. At times he felt forced to bend the truth -well, to lie, a white lie -for "business reasons." He felt stress in what he was doing. I know so much about this young man because I was that man.
>
> I really didn't like to do what I was more and more being asked to do. I'd try to put down that nagging little voice of conscience by justifying myself. The more I felt that inner rebellion, the more I felt trapped by what I was doing.
>
> The struggle, not too unlike Jacob's, put an increasing mental burden on me. So much so that my back, physically, began to hurt under the strain. One time, for example, it took me twenty minutes to walk just a block and a half from my office to my

car. And for three years I went to one doctor after another trying to get relief.

The last constructed a brace for me. It fitted up under my shoulders and went down over my hips. I had to wear it more and more -taking it off before I'd go to sleep and putting it on before I got up. I was also told I should have an operation.

During this time one of the people who called on me at my office began to leave copies of the daily newspaper she represented, *The Christian Science Monitor*. I'd wait 'til she was gone and drop them into the waste basket. This went on for a year, until finally I began to read that newspaper.

There's a short article about God in every issue. I began to read that, too. Then as I'd go out in my job through airports and bus terminals other Christian Science literature -like the weekly *Christian Science Sentinel* - would catch my eye. And now and then I'd pick up copies and read them, too.

Well, one day my back seemed particularly bad. When I got to my desk, I sat there holding on to some thought about God I'd just been reading. God as support - my support and everyone's. I suddenly felt compelled to take off the brace. I rode home that night in less discomfort with the brace off than I had coming in with it on. The next morning I woke up and didn't have any pain at all. It was like waking up from a bad dream - a dream I suddenly saw I didn't have to go along with anymore.

Glen finished recounting this healing experience by saying, "The real you and the real me is healthy and whole and free all the time. Instead of having to go along with a burdened self, each of us is spiritually whole and free."

I later found out a little more background information about this remarkable healing. When he woke up that morning without pain, Glen actually ran up and down the stairs in his home waiting for the pain to return, which it didn't. And the one leg that had become so drawn up that he needed a lift in his shoe was restored to its normal length. The burden of wrong-doing was literally crippling him, so his freedom involved much more than removing an uncomfortable brace. That brings us to another subject, though perhaps not a very popular one.

What about sin?

The "white lies" that Glen told in business to cover his tracks gave him a problem. He knew it was wrong. This activity falls under a heading that has somewhat lost favor with us today as being either too religious, too harsh or too judgmental. The heading or category is "sin." The dictionary simply defines sin as an offense against religious or moral law. Today, with more emphasis placed on civil law than on God's law and with current attempts to be politically correct, we might be more apt to label such a person, "morally challenged."

A few days after writing the above sentence (a little tongue-in-cheek I must admit) a television news channel carried the story of a group of people who had knowingly committed a crime against a certain sector of society. However, the news caption simply stated, "Ethically challenged." It didn't label them sinners or criminals, just challenged as to their ethics. Perhaps the people who felt victimized by their actions would not agree!

Years ago, I heard that the word "sin" was an old archery term meaning to "miss the mark." Older dictionaries add the word, "*voluntarily*." A mistake is an error. If I step squarely on your toes, thinking they are merely a bump on the floor, while passing your seat in a narrow theater row, I am in error. But this error, because it is painful and distressing, constitutes an evil, an evil which has befallen you due to my neglect. However, if I knowingly step on your toes—and even enjoy doing it—then we are talking about sin.

An Eartha Kitt song, many years ago, went something like this, "And when I'm in the theater I want to change my seat just so I can step on everybody's feet." The main theme was, "I want to be evil, little evil me, just as evil as I can be." Well, I think it should have been "little sinful me" but perhaps my correction would not be appreciated!

Certain habits that were once classified in the "sin" category have, over the last decade or so, been moved into the "sickness" column. But just how helpful would it be to a pedestrian or a bus driver to tell them they are sick when they are actually going the wrong way? We are told that Jesus cast seven (unspecified) devils out of Mary Magdalene (Mark 16:9). Without seeming to make light of our current efforts at compassion, it might be worth noting that in today's reclassified world, this could translate into five sicknesses and two devils.

Sickness may slow us down or speed us on our journey, all depending on how we handle it—as an opportunity to prove God's goodness, or as a load to carry. Sin, on the other hand, always takes us off the path. The same Principle heals both, but the classification on our spiritual path is different—just as airports, freeways, and dead-ends are properly classified on road maps.

In their healing ministries, prophets and apostles comforted the sick but often had strong, awakening words for the sinner. Jesus had stated, "I came not to call the righteous, but sinners to repentance," (Luke 5:32). He was turning around those traveling in a wrong direction, but not those traveling in a good direction. However, even the correctly-positioned travelers still have to deal with off-track thinking all the time!

Like a heaven-bound rocket, our spiritual trajectory needs careful monitoring. Life is not a static event. If it were, then no guidance—human or divine—would be necessary, as you can't guide a stationary object. Plainly, we do need guidance and daily answers, and for two reasons. There are external and internal influences that would divert us. Media newscasts, the plethora of advertising or the tide of human opinion will all too easily drag an unwary swimmer in life's ocean out of the safety zone, enticing them into unwitting errors or committing wilful sin.

One who is falsely influenced, hypnotized in a sense, to believe that committing a wrong, a minus activity, can lead to a plus life is actually working against his own best interests and those of society in general. Wrong-doing is always against the perpetrator though it may be aimed at another. It's a boomerang! One can't win by those means. (A disoriented football player, running in the wrong direction, can't score points for his team by making a touchdown over his own goal line.) No wonder olden-time preachers thundered at such individuals to repent and get off the path that leads to self-destruction.

Unfortunately, the dire prediction of eternal damnation often accompanied the warning. There was no promise of a possible U-turn in the afterlife. But how could God's love cease at a physical horizon or boundary line, for it is as eternal and infinite as God who is Love itself? The license plate frame that reads, "God allows U-turns" could have added one word, "God *forever* allows U-turns." An individual always has the opportunity for reform, but why put it off till later, why not now? (This subject will be discussed further in Part Two of this book).

Remember the statement Glen made in his lecture: "The real you and the real me is healthy and whole and free all the time. Instead of having to go along with a burdened self, each of us is spiritually whole and free." Well, the same is true about us and sin. Our true selves in the image and likeness of God are pure and sinless according to the first chapter of Genesis where God saw everything that he had made and it was very good.

This is what we are proving on our spiritual journey. And we shouldn't be surprised if errors or sins stand out to us and become very apparent along the way. This is the second point—that of internal influences. We'll find off-track thinking to deal with in ourselves, and others, just as a good mathematician will quickly recognize mental math mistakes and deal with them. The clearer we become spiritually, the more obvious will be the subtle sins. It's a sign of good progress if we find ourselves faced with the "just-how-I-am" bunch. Such untoward characteristics as temper, arrogance, and self-righteousness will become all too evident, and we'll have to eradicate them in order to stay on track.

The righteous who are not alert and don't notice these telltale signs of sin along the way will be deluded into thinking they have arrived too soon and may even forget they are on a spiritual journey home. Such individuals are content with a type of human goodness without progress—a self-deceived state that merely ambles along pleasantly but unthinkingly. It's a form of infidelity to a high purpose. While we continue to believe in (and experience) mortal life, variable love, and uncertain truth there is still a journey to be made, individually and collectively.

37

The saddest of all wars.

A wrong influence could extend to a large group of people just as easily as to an individual. Illusionists entertain by convincing an entire audience to believe in something that's truly impossible. That seems rather harmless but what about a wrong path that's taken en masse? A whole nation might be mentally influenced to dominate others or terrorize them. That's called war.

The saddest of all wars, so I used to think, was civil war where one brother is pitted against another, but this surely takes second place to the war which began in the 1960s where young people, usually the best and brightest of our young men (sometimes women too), were recruited to make war on their parents. "Don't trust anyone over thirty, especially your parents!" was the slogan as all authority was challenged. Even siblings in agreement with parents were viewed as being on the side of "the enemy."

Of course, parents weren't perfect. What human parent is? That parental perfection is reserved for God, but even our heavenly Parent came under attack. Bumper stickers carried the message "God is dead." At least that brought bumper-sticker rebuttal, "My God is alive, sorry about yours!"

But the tidal wave against parents continued and swept across nations leaving the debris of broken families and broken hearts in its wake! Who won the war? In 1998, a sign displayed in a restaurant section, designed to appeal to children's tastes, simply and rather comically stated, "Kids rule!"

In declaring the winner of this war, it was evident that everyone had lost. Children lost the protection and guidance that would naturally be afforded them by the many parents who do care about their children. The parents increasingly lost control of their children, even unaware that their offspring were planning to run amok in a school yard with firearms. Yes, the fallout from the war on parents lies like atomic waste scattered over the juvenile landscape of today.

A couple of years ago, I invited a woman, who was signing me up on the telephone for a business service, to come to lunch at my home. She had recently lost her mother and was sad. We sat at the table for over five hours touching on many subjects, spending much time on one in particular. Her brother, now in his fifties, was still railing against her and both of his departed parents. We talked about the war on parents and how it affected everyone in the family. That generation was high, if not on drugs (which were rampant) certainly on the self-absorbing idea of liberating themselves from personal constraints or duties. Today, it has even been suggested by some of that generation that they never grew up.

After discussing this subject, I believe my visitor left with some level of comfort and understanding. She saw that her brother was not in this war alone, that it was not his own individual plan being carried out. Rather, it was a mass mental influence that had taken over the youth.

A year later, I was speaking by phone to a woman in another country who told me the same story. Her brother even accused her of taking their parents' money as she kept meticulous accounts of expenditures in caring for them in their later years while he was still off in mental Never Land being angry at all of them.

When he finally settled down a little at about sixty years of age (the parents by this time had gone) she told him she was glad that whatever it was—the difficulty that had been between the two of them—had now vanished. She said he looked at her startled and shook himself, but replied with total lack of recognition, "What! What was that? What are you talking about?" He doesn't realize to this day just what did go on for all those lost years.

Though often aimed at both parents, sometimes the chosen target was the greater authority figure—usually the father. The ammunition in this war on parents was any parental infraction, imaginary or real, which was magnified beyond belief as the youth protested faulty advice given them or simple requests to perform a service such as wash the family car. But these youths were in a different service. Everyone was wrong except the recruit (the hypnotized one).

The youth didn't stop to reflect that they were in actual fact saying, "If you want to know how bad my parents really are, just look at me, their product!" Sadly, they also didn't realize they were being influenced to fight against the very ones they should have trusted most, the ones who loved them and who had literally fought for them during WWII. Yes, their parents were part of what Tom Brokaw in his book named "The Greatest Generation."

Some people today are even oblivious to the fact that this war took place. A friend told me she had no idea what went on with the youth in that era as she was busy in her own little world raising small children. But in my work (which I'll talk about later) I was receiving calls from parents and hearing incredible stories that even included threats of physical abuse. Anger at parents is like kicking out the rung below you on a ladder. It doesn't make much sense and there's no gratitude for what the rung has provided.

Though it took me nearly thirty years to figure out to my own satisfaction what took place during the sixties, this still leaves the quiet question with me and obviously with society in general of how best to handle the situation at this point and diffuse the danger from that fallout. Prayer is an obvious answer, so is sharing helpful ideas with each other. I, for one, would love to talk with the parents of today and apologize for those in my generation. Yes, even on behalf of those who did not participate in the war on parents. We just couldn't stop what was going on because we, ourselves, were clueless as to what was happening.

Divine Love is the most powerful solution (both as an answer and a solvent), because it dissolves whatever is unlike itself. Expressing God who is Love in daily life makes us increasingly kind, infinitely gentle and spiritually strong. While this love may appear as the tender cradling of an individual starving themselves under the influence of current bodily fashions, it may also show itself in the tough love that rehabilitates a drug addict. And divine Love will answer our prayers as to how we can best help the unwitting recruits of the war on parents for, in a way, they were the worst casualties of that war.

But there are hopeful stirrings evident today among parents and in society, even in current advertisements on television such as the one declaring that to know where your kids are is not prying—it's parenting. Perhaps parental rights and duties are creeping back into vogue. Let's hope and pray for that to happen because the wise commandment to honor our father and our mother has never been more needed. John, the beloved disciple of Jesus, asked a leading question, "he who loves not his brother whom he hath seen, how can he love God whom he hath not seen? And along these lines, perhaps a timely question would be, "If we don't love and honor the parent that we do see, how can we love and honor the Parent that we don't see?"

When still in the process of writing this section I enjoyed a few words outside a supermarket with a young man, built like a football player, who loaded the groceries into my car. I asked him how long he'd worked at the store and was surprised when he answered eleven years. I told him he looked more like a college student, at which he smiled broadly and said, "That's 'cause I listen to my Mama. I look younger and don't have any stress, because I listen to my Mama." He respects his mother. And I have a strong hunch that she respects him too. Yes, the tide must be turning! The wrong direction can't win. Sin can't win.

However, sin on an individual or collective scale is not a happy topic. Do we really have to talk about the subject at all? Yes, because without facing it, the problem won't be solved. There's also another reason. It is virtually impossible to discuss prayer and quiet answers without discussing sin.

Prayer, fueled by love for God and man, is the vehicle that takes us to divine Love, in the direction of all that's truly good—to lasting feelings of worth and satisfaction, permanent joy, brotherly love, health and peace (how heavenly!).

On the other hand, sin is a vehicle, fueled by toxic chemicals (emotions), that takes one away in the opposite direction—to fleeting pleasures, worthlessness, degradation, disease, unsatisfied yearnings, broken relationships, bitter disappointments and perpetual pain (talk about hell!). So it's not surprising that there are many references to sin in the Bible (and in the chapter on prayer, found in a wonderful Bible reference book that I'll speak about later).

For now, let's go to the lighter side of making U-turns. Even what appears to be a small character flaw requires a U-turn of one kind or another. As the saying goes, "You can't be just a little bit pregnant." And it's hard to be just a little bit prideful. Either you are or you're not!

What happened to my chauffeur?

When I was a teenager, living in Holland, my mother joined me there so we could travel together by train to meet my Dad who worked for UNICEF in Paris. (Yes, he was the man who saw the travel poster.) Our family had gone through a number of challenging situations and so this promised to be a wonderful adventure—at least in the simpler world of the mid-1950s it certainly was.

My dad expected to meet us at the train station in Paris with a chauffeur-driven car, flowers for my mother and candy for me. So, with much anticipation and with the confidence that often suddenly descends on teenagers, I took charge of the expedition. As we hurried up the steps of the station, with me in the lead of course, the announcement rang out that the train for Paris was leaving from the second platform.

After some months of living in the country and being rather sure of my ability to understand and speak Dutch, I informed my mother and we made our way to the second platform and onto the train. We enjoyed the trip as the train chugged along, until arriving in Amsterdam where a kind man offered to take down our luggage for us. I told him not to bother, that we were going to Paris. "Not on this train," he replied,"this is the end of the line."

In my smugness, I had neglected to notice that there were two sides to the second platform and that the train to Paris had actually departed in the opposite direction. A little more humility and a tad more geography would have been helpful!

So there we were in the middle of the night in a city that was almost closed down. But a quiet answer was still available. My grandfather lived in Amsterdam so we made our way to his townhouse and knocked vigorously on the door. In his sleepy state, my grandfather seemed to think that Holland was under invasion and spoke to us from an upper window in various languages until we were able to persuade him it was safe to let us in. After a short night draped over a couple of chairs, we returned to the station and finally took the train to Paris. Only this time there was no chauffeur that I can recall, and I'm not totally sure anymore about the flowers and candy. But my dad was there.

Even a little pride can send one off on a wild goose chase. It diminishes our capacity to make good judgments, to reason things out. Pride, imbued with its own expertise and abilities, forgets to mention where they came from; like a lamp saying it can light up on its own without a connection to a power source or a TV claiming to broadcast a program without a signal being sent to it.

The Paris trip was a good lesson and I was glad we could all laugh about it. So, again the Bible was right. Pride, or haughtiness, not only "goeth before a fall," but I can testify to the fact that pride also goeth before the wrong train!

However, the pride U-turn is a rather slow one to make, so I've found over the years. Just as you think it's been accomplished, it becomes obvious one has made only a wide-angle turn and there's more distance to travel.

When less is more.

Many years ago, I was talking with a group of people who were giving their various opinions on some point. After waiting quite patiently (and humbly I might add) for everyone to finish, I spoke up. "Now let's look at this the right way!" (Meaning my way, of course!) I still smile and grimace at the same time about that one. But then it's easier to laugh outright at another's lapse in humility. I recall a woman who told me in all sweet sincerity, "Now dear, there's no one more humble than I, but . . ." as she proceeded to complain about someone who was evidently less humble.

The attempt to justify ourselves, to explain what we did and why, so that someone else gets the "right" idea of us, is usually a futile effort. And what makes us do that? Remember the old line, "the devil made me do it?" Yes, it's probably the little devil of pride that prompts us in these directions. I don't by any means claim total exemption, but spiritual growth over a period of time has helped to some degree. This poem, written a few years ago, is part of my journey.

Good Justification

So others would not think badly of me
I tried now and then to prove
That what I had been doing
Was something they would approve.

A well-placed word
A little phrase
Should show me
Not too far from praise.

And it also worked, or so I thought
That my standing was kept intact
By a meaningful explanation
Of some little-known fact.

But light years later I'm finding
That which makes me satisfied
Is the God-directed doing of good
For by *these* works we are justified.

So, now it's of no great import
What comments about me may be,
Not because I think less about others,
But because I think less about me.

A local church displaying spiritually-pointed sayings on its large sign carried this message: "Humility is not thinking less of yourself but thinking of yourself less!"

Isn't that great! Of course, the "less" is different in both of these instances. The first "less" means **quality** of thought, thinking poorly, badly of yourself—which we are **not** required to do. The second "less" points to **quantity** of thought devoted to oneself (the meaning in the poem above). This is where the requirement kicks in.

The very popular "You have to love yourself" concept can be helpful if it persuades one to give up poor thoughts about oneself, or about anyone for that matter. But the same saying is not useful if it is construed to mean quantity of thinking, focusing more often on oneself. If interest is a good determiner of love then someone who is very interested in themselves (good or bad) already possesses a large portion of self-love. But this is quantity not quality and needs to be replaced with humility and a genuine appreciation for all the good expressed by oneself or another.

It may sound strange, but I've found it to be true, that an individual drowning in the deep waters of chronic self-dislike needs the lifesaver of humility just as much as the egotist encountering rocks while swimming in the shallows of self-satisfaction. The former believes that they cannot reach the high noon of their being and are perpetually unworthy. The latter believes they are a superlative form of being, who has, in effect, gone beyond high noon, more perfect than perfection. Neither scenario is accurate. It's a script written for and by the human ego, which casts itself in the starring role of either good or bad guy. Not terribly important which role, as long as the ego is the star.

Goodbye, ego!

The human ego badly needs a replacement part called humility. (Now try to manufacture that in a petri dish or by cloning!) The human ego somehow believes itself to be the central sun around which all the other planets (all you guys out there!) revolve. It's the "me-and-my-universe" complex. The rethinking of centrality is a required course on our spiritual journey. Locating the sun as center of the solar system instead of the earth was scientific progress. Spiritual progress involves acknowledging the Principle of all true being, God, as central to our spiritual universe. This universe must have a center just as the spokes on a bicycle wheel require a hub.

"I AM" is how God revealed Himself to Moses when setting the patriarch out on the demanding assignment to liberate the children of Israel. Concerned with his speaking ability, Moses was at first rebuked for not understanding that the divine power was the source of all human abilities. Then he was reassured that the needed help was at hand. Aaron would function as spokesman and go with him.

Interesting isn't it that Moses was not given a "you-can-do-this-yourself" message. Either Moses would have not been open to it, or perhaps Aaron was a better solution and would enable Moses to stay on the humble side of greatness. Obedience and much humility would be requisite for such an immense undertaking.

The liberation of the children of Israel from bondage also required such an alignment with our heavenly Principle that Moses was given special instructions for his journey that would apply to ours also. He was given the Ten Commandments. This was not a mission for the spiritually weak or for the egotist. God—the divine Ego—needed to be central and solo, not duplicated. The one divine Ego may be reflected by man, but it cannot be split off into a bunch of little egocentric beings—little spokes all functioning on their own. Try to ride that bike!

Right where a limited, mortal man, woman or child appears to be, right there instead of that limited edition of creation is the true, spiritual child of God and a more spiritual view enables us to gain at least a glimpse of what that might entail. To recognize oneself spiritually as a child of God and see others in the same light is foundational to humility and to real satisfaction.

Humility happily accepts a subordinate position in a legitimate situation as in business or in the military. But a false subordination is not meekness. True humility is bowing to the divine will rather than submissiveness to another's will. In other words and in plain language, we are not required to be a doormat! Doing God's will, and discerning carefully between His will and human will or opinion, is part of the navigational equipment necessary for a spiritual journey.

Pick him up! Put him down!

People's opinions as to what we should or shouldn't do may vary widely. The following incident is still vivid in memory. As a young mother, I was walking through a department store with my little boy, of about two years of age, who was pulling at my skirt, wanting to be picked up. It might be well to note at this point, he was a rather big, little boy so I wasn't too eager to accommodate. However, a friend suddenly appeared in front of us and with compassion for the toddler commiserated, "Poor little thing. Pick him up and carry him." So I gave in, scooped up my big bundle and staggered off into the elevator.

As the doors opened on the next floor, I found myself facing another acquaintance who took one quick look at us and immediately, emphatically proclaimed, "That big lump! Put him down and make him walk on his own two feet!" Yes, two very well-meaning individuals with totally opposite advice. That's why it's necessary to listen for quiet answers. Oh, we may even take another's advice but we need more than human opinion. We need to feel the divine Spirit moving us. We need heaven's nod to the situation. We need to ask the quiet question and listen for the quiet answer.

Though we may relinquish, to a marked degree, attempts to live up to what another expects, there are still our own ideals to contend with; ideals that are sometimes well nigh impossible and impractical. A little boy is not going to be Superman. A woman may not be a supermom able to juggle just about everything that comes her way. In fact we may even fail at the small expectations we have for ourselves and for one good reason. There's often too much of us in them. Too much self! We may even be surprised to find out one hot day that our proposed unselfish deed promises us a starring role. So do we accept it?

The lemonade queen.

It seemed like a perfectly reasonable and good way to help others. A van, carrying a household cleaning crew, broke down opposite my home. The man in charge of the group, who couldn't speak English, had phoned for a back-up van but it was slow in arriving. A small tree didn't afford much shade from the hot sun so I decided to take a trayload of drinks over to them. Happily, I began pouring out lemonade while I anticipated their joy. Then I found myself hoping the van would not arrive until I had made my entrance with the tray. Now, let's think about that for a moment. Which do you suspect those people really hoped for—my cool lemonade or an air-conditioned vehicle? Not a difficult choice! The vision of myself floating across the street coming to their rescue like some Lady Bountiful (a phrase I'd heard growing up) was my own scenario of goodness.

Well, I did deliver the drinks and the group was able to enjoy them just before the van arrived, but it taught me a little lesson. If good deeds bring more tears to our own eyes than to the eyes of the person receiving them—in other words, if we are more touched at the thought of our helpfulness than the individual being helped—then it's time to rethink the deed or our motive and attitude in doing it! It's difficult to hear real solutions or quiet answers with "my song," the melody of self-love, playing in the background of consciousness.

The walk of fame or the road to true satisfaction?

Perhaps our many expectations of ourselves need to be rethought quite frequently. For instance, the little boy who wants to be Superman or an action hero could be encouraged to do super-deeds of kindness. And the busy mom or businesswoman might employ greater wisdom as to what she expects. Her good works may include fewer schedules for her family or for herself.

Doing one's duty, unselfishly and lovingly, does bring strength and happiness, but simply attempting to carry out our own ideals or what the world expects of us is burdensome. Jesus meekly and humbly carried out his duty, the will of the Father. What a different perspective on life! No wonder he beckoned us, "Come unto me, all ye that labour and are heavy laden, and I will give you rest. Take my yoke upon you, and learn of me; for I am meek and lowly in heart: and ye shall find rest unto your souls. For my yoke is easy and my burden is light" (Matt.11:28). How needed this is, in today's busy world!

Interestingly, we never need to justify ourselves because there is something that does it for us. Our works in life either justify us (show we are on the right track, conforming to what is just and good) or these works condemn us (show the opposite).

But the quiet justification of quiet deeds does not always, unfortunately, satisfy the human desire to feel valuable in the world's eyes. We want to feel validated. We desire the rubber-stamp of public endorsement and approval. In a way, it's a little like getting our parking stub validated by a business for taking up space in their garage. But, do we really need the world's validation for taking up space on this planet? The world is very changeable, quite fickle, so *what* or *who* is popular today is either on the trash heap or is a "has been" tomorrow. How valuable can that be?

Jesus was quite unmoved by popularity or persecution and, regardless of whether the crowd was trying to push him over a hill or crown him king, still went about His Father's business. He received little to no validation from the world. He was not going to get a star on the sidewalk of fame. But he knew he had the highest approval rating possible. After humbly allowing himself to be baptized by John, Jesus heard this heavenly message, "This is my beloved Son, in whom I am well pleased" (Matthew 3:17). But even prior to this, Jesus knew, at only twelve years of age, that he had to be about his Father's business.

At some point we'll all have to come to that recognition and make that conscious decision too, because it's part of going home spiritually. It's also part of losing stress at work. Just as we need to identify ourselves as children of God, we also need to make a better business connection. And being in this business doesn't necessarily require leaving our human occupation.

Usually any child has easy access to the family business. No long forms to fill out or troublesome interviews. No "don't call me, I'll call you." If we acknowledge God as our Father then His business is open to us too. To be about our Father's business doesn't involve years of college, hi-tech abilities or genius.

This family business is based on two things: being and doing good. It's that simple. And we don't have to wait for others to free up their calendars because we can transact this business anywhere, anytime. It can be accomplished at the grocery store, the post office or a business board room, but perhaps the best place to start is at home.

"Charity begins at home" is a great motto but often the store clerk receives more appreciation than a family member. That can quickly change by a simple change of attitude. Two friends of mine told me, within days of each other, that they had decided to appreciate the ones in their household instead of waiting for circumstances or people to change.

One woman looked for and quickly recognized just how appreciated she was although previously she had felt totally unappreciated. She said even a simple "thank you" was evidence of how valued she was. Another woman acknowledged that her husband was actually doing the best he could and with that she relaxed into the appreciation mode. She was no longer waiting for him to make her happy.

Both of these individuals found out that invisible good was actually quite tangible and more present than they had imagined. How satisfying to be about the Father's business! It produces great dividends and helps pave and pay for our way home.

Taking the high road home.

One of the first commands that Christ Jesus preached on his redemptive and healing mission was, " Repent: for the kingdom of heaven is at hand" (Matthew 4:17). The original meaning of "repent" was to turn back or to rethink, so Jesus' rebukes were not for the purpose of accusation but out of love to aid the spiritual traveler. He pointed them in a better direction.

The young advertising executive who rethought his direction become so known for his high ethics that a prospective business partner suggested to him, " Say, Glen, you take the high road, I'll take the low road and we'll get 'em in the middle." Needless to say, Glen declined the partnership and not long afterwards went into the full-time practice of spiritual healing. He knew he was on a spiritual journey.

His U-turn had a lasting effect on others' lives, healing them, including raising the dying, over the many years he practiced. It's interesting too that on the way to his healing practice he actually became the National Advertising Manager for the newspaper that he had tossed into the waste-basket for a whole year. His answer was waiting for him and no matter how many times he tossed it aside, the answer was not going to disappear. Glen's gratitude for a new life took the form of helping others live anew, with health, harmony and a better direction.

Let us make our U-turns, great or small, with much gratitude. All such U-turns are totally legal and we'll receive, instead of a traffic ticket, a divine commendation for making them. How wonderful that, wherever we are on our individual pathway, God's law always allows for U-turns!

It's Who You Know. It Really Is!

It takes work to progress in the line of spiritual discovery. For instance, just to accept that there is a perfect Principle to whom we may take our questions is a leap of faith for many. But to advance from blind faith to a reasoned faith and from there to an understanding of God requires persistent effort and prayer. "..With all thy getting get understanding" the Book of Proverbs (4:7) counsels. So, that's how Glen came to be sitting in his closet. It was to "get understanding."

Prayer in the closet.

Jesus had counseled, "But thou, when thou prayest, enter into thy closet, and when thou hast shut thy door, pray to thy Father which is in secret; and thy Father which seeth in secret shall reward thee openly" (Matthew 6:6). Of course, Glen realized that Jesus didn't literally mean a closet but a quiet mental state where you could shut out all the material evidence being presented against the spiritual facts of being. After that wonderful healing, Glen wanted to know God better and this was the only quiet place he could find to study, think and pray. With deep yearning he would write questions on a pad, questions such as, "How good is God?" and, " How infinite is the infinite?" And he would receive answers to these questions.

As he told me about this closet study years later, Glen said that after learning more about God and God's goodness, he found those early answers that had come to him were still correct. Yes, infinite Spirit is present in every corner of the globe, present for every race and religion. There is no question we cannot take to our heavenly Parent for an answer. It truly is a matter of "who you

57

know." Now, I must mention that the book often quoted in *The Christian Science Sentinel* articles Glen had read (the book that had unlocked the Bible's healing power for him) is the same book that was introduced to me as a child.

A quiet discovery.

Over the years, I've consistently found this book to be the most illuminating companion, resource or reference book to the Bible. It was written by a New England woman in the nineteenth century and it's called *Science and Health with Key to the Scriptures.* With early widowhood, a child taken from her, a failed second marriage to a philandering dentist and chronic ill-health, this woman was impelled to search the Scriptures for answers. Having come from a strongly religious family, as many families were in her day, this was a natural recourse to her. And through quiet yearning and sincere, spiritual striving she received a wonderful revelation.

At the time of what promised to be a fatal accident, spiritual light was poured onto the pages of the Bible and they became illumined to her. She gained new spiritual insight into a healing that Jesus had performed. She then arose from what others, including her attending physician, considered to be her death bed and her sought-after healing came quickly. She pursued this revelation and found the spiritual laws behind the wonderful healings Jesus accomplished, enabling her to follow him with striking results in the healing work which he urges upon all of us.

Mary Baker Eddy knew this was not a human philosophy or some vague theory that she herself had formulated. Just as Marie Curie discovered radium and Isaac Newton propounded laws of gravity, Mary Baker Eddy had made a discovery. But it was not in the line of physical science though it was a new, old science she had found. She had discovered divine Science, laws of God that had existed forever. She found that God is the Principle of these laws which were understood and practiced to perfection by Christ Jesus for humanity's sake. So Mrs. Eddy named her discovery Christian Science.

The quiet answers this woman received have had very open results and rewards in the healing of countless people, my family included. Many are healed as they read her book looking for answers. The Bible has become a practical, open and understood chart of life because of this discovery which throws light on biblical concepts in practical, spiritually-scientific terms.

For instance, the Christ, as explained in Christian Science is the divine nature of God, which we all must express. It is the truth of all of God's children, made in His image and likeness. Jesus was not the sole possessor of that nature, though he was the highest demonstrator of it the world has ever known. We may say of an individual that they are "kindness itself" but we don't mean that no one else can be kind. "Honest Abe" was a title given to Abraham Lincoln but honesty was not his alone. In the same way, Christ is the invisible, divine idea of God, and is the title given to Jesus who was the human expression or representative of that idea.

Understanding this distinction of the human and the divine, of Jesus and the Christ, enables us to follow in Jesus' footsteps, otherwise the path—the way—would be out of sight. The Christ is the divine way and Jesus is the human Way-shower. The Christ is the divine message sent to us and Jesus is the human messenger who lived the message. With his pure beginning, being born of a virgin, Jesus was more than humanly equipped for his mission.

That this Christ, Truth, existed long before Jesus arrived, is obvious in a statement Paul made about Moses. He was talking about the faith (a favorite topic of Paul's) of Moses as he left the riches of Egypt, "Esteeming the reproach of Christ greater riches than the treasures in Egypt . . ." (Hebrews 11:26). Now Moses lived fifteen hundred years before Jesus, so Paul in making that statement had to have recognized that the Christ pre-dated Jesus. Surely Paul was saying how much better it is to live in a difficult situation going the right way, the way of the Christ, than to live amidst sinful pleasures of the flesh, going the wrong way.

Speaking of understanding timeless biblical truths, it would not be possible for me to write this book or discuss this subject were it not for the understanding of the Bible which *Science and Health* provides. No one writes in a vacuum but from their own background of experience, and this is mine. The explanations as to how to hear the quiet answers, why we sometimes don't hear, and other related topics may be conclusions arrived at through prayer and practical experience but all have the foundational support and guidance of the Bible and its divine Science as explained in Christian Science.

Prayer is the beginning of spiritual answers and that's exactly where *Science and Health* begins, with the chapter "Prayer." Only seventeen pages long, it deals with many important aspects of the subject and would be a beneficial addition to anyone's reading list.

A well-kept secret.

One hundred and twenty-six years after its first printing in 1875, this book sold its ten millionth copy and yet so many have never heard of it. With it only now becoming more visible we might well ask: Why has this book been such a well-kept secret? In the beginning *Science and Health* traveled by word of mouth as people recommended it for healing. And heal it did! But objections arose to this Christian method of treating disease and the chapter "Some Objections Answered" was later added to the book. Furthermore, the author's biblically-based explanation of God as Life, Truth, Love, Spirit, with the addition of Soul, Mind and Principle, did not sit well with religious views of the era. A God who was vengeful—a selective God or a man in the sky with a long white beard—was light years away from the Supreme Being who is divine Love.

Perhaps a fortress mentality began to grow alongside the organization that spread in the wake of the discovery and the founding of Christian Science. "Let's pull up the drawbridge and prevent any attacks" might seem like good protection. Nothing can get in. The only problem is that nothing can get out either. It is quite understandable that many became increasingly wary about recommending a book that differed from the strongly conservative religious views or popular scientific theories of those times.

I remember as a child being taught, probably in 1950, that "an atom is the smallest part of matter and cannot be divided." Yes, it still rolls easily off the tongue though it has long been disproved. But now we're talking about a book that was an atom smasher, spiritually speaking, long before the Fermi Lab took on even one atom. Here was a discovery that peered into matter and saw *nothing*! As *Science and Health* states, "Matter disappears under the microscope of Spirit" (p. 264). Though the book was plainly ahead of its time that still didn't change the impact on lives that were healed and reformed.

Doubtless, one of the reasons for resisting Christian Science was the fact that the discovery was made by a woman. A research paper revealed one religious view of women in the mid-1800s. Theologians of that time (the time of Mary Baker Eddy) were still trying to ascertain whether or not a woman had a soul. Now, some groups are hoping to find out whether or not a carrot has a soul.

That's quite a mental distance to have traveled, isn't it! But, the only reason we can look back at past customs and be amazed is because progress has been made. For every advancing step, surely it would be better to say, "Look at how far we've come, that something like that seems so untenable today!" Yes, we can *look back* with gratitude and *look forward* to even greater social and spiritual progress.

Increasingly, the golden thread of love is being woven into the fabric of society as we deal with equality issues in many areas. History books showing the advancing steps of humanity towards a more humane civilization should fill students with appreciation and inspire them to do better. Looking back would then serve instructional goals rather than feed negative emotions.

Now, it is necessary to state, from an historical standpoint, that the former strictly-defined role and status of women would account in part for the cover-up of the book *Science and Health*.

A woman did what?

One look at the full title of her book, *Science and Health with Key to the Scriptures,* reveals that Mary Baker Eddy had entered into three prominent fields, those of science, theology and medicine—fields that were almost exclusively populated by men. A cookbook certainly would have been more acceptable.

However, women of her day were stirring the pot of freedom, yearning to taste a liberation they had never before known. Her contemporaries Susan B. Anthony and Elizabeth Cady Stanton were laboring long and hard for female suffrage, even as Mary Baker Eddy toiled to bring the higher freedom from sickness and disease to all mankind. By the time all women in the United States had gained the vote in 1920 (fifty years after the amendment had been passed to include all males, regardless of race), *Science and Health* had already spent nearly a half century traveling the globe. It surged, like an army of one, across the front lines of troubled thought, doing battle with entrenched beliefs and liberating thousands from the yoke of despair, sickness, lack and the multitudinous evils that seem to befall humanity.

However, there was no ticker tape parade in store for this Christian soldier, clad in its literary battle dress by a woman. Sick bodies yielded to health far more quickly through the reading of *Science and Health* than did doubts as to the viability and capability of women. That Glen had to deal with misgivings about a woman's contribution was frankly and honestly stated in his first lecture, "Let Your Basis Be Love."

He even referred to himself in that lecture as a male chauvinist, a term that gained popularity in the 1960s. Here is part of what he had to say:

I once had a strong bias against women. As a male, I felt I couldn't be told anything of moment or value by a woman. There's a prejudice for you! You can imagine the peace that one gave me! And on top of that, as you know, Mary Baker Eddy founded Christian Science. Since she was a woman—well, you can see the problem I had. Of course, my male prejudice didn't start with Mrs. Eddy. Apparently, it stemmed from my acceptance of the generally-held belief of male superiority. And this, in turn, was rooted in the false premise of a 'partial' God—a God that would give one more good than another. As long as I held to the belief of a God who played favorites, I was prejudicing my whole view of man—man in the image of God, absolute, spiritual Love.

Glen also stated he had a bias against reading the Bible. Having experienced that marvelous healing of a crippling back condition, he gained new respect for the Scriptures because Christian Science, the Science that healed him, was based on the Scriptures. He was finding that the divine Spirit, the Supreme Being, needed to be understood. It wasn't a matter of blind faith in any religion but a spiritual understanding that was needed, and it was right within his reach.

This divine Principle, he found, operated everywhere for everyone. It certainly didn't apply only to a certain group of people, to a particular religion or to only one gender. Glen went on in his lecture to recount how his prejudice against women dissolved as he began to realize just what Mary Baker Eddy had accomplished.

Here was a woman with what had to be some of the greatest courage I'd ever even considered. Imagine presenting a book like *Science and Health* to the world, a world so set in its way, a world filled with prejudice and resistance—even open attacks on anything new, let alone, radical. I began to glimpse the love Mrs. Eddy must have felt for this world, and my own petty prejudices dissolved. It took fearless love, real courage, to bring out this book with its revolutionary premise—that God, Spirit, is All. Infinite. And wholly good. That His creation, man is like unto Himself—perfect, spiritual, and whole. And, therefore, that evil and the limitations of matter have no part in Love's creation.

It was only as I typed these words that I realized Glen himself had courage to confess, so honestly, his former prejudice against women to large audiences in the early 1970s. That was an era filled with strong advocates, and sometimes strident voices, for the women's rights movement.

The radio interview.

It was just as well Glen reconciled his thoughts about women because he was going to meet all kinds of prejudice in various speaking capacities. At one time (before I knew him), probably close to 1970, he was invited to be interviewed on the radio. For some reason he felt it was important to be there early. So he arrived at the radio station with about an hour to spare.

The subject was going to be Christian Science and Glen expected an interested and fair inquiry to take place. The interviewer, however, obviously had something quite different in mind. As the two men sat down for a pre-interview chat, it quickly became apparent that the interviewer had already made up his mind to tear this young man to shreds, verbally speaking, as soon as they aired. He felt quite antagonistic to what he thought Christian Science was.

However, as they talked, the question as to the nature of God arose and the interviewer expressed the opinion that no one would be able to speak more than a few minutes on that subject. Glen then explained his expanded view of God, due to his study of Christian Science. The minutes ticked by as he told of the divine Love that meets all human needs. Finally, he paused. The interviewer looked at him incredulously and said something to the effect that anyone who had such a full and practical knowledge of God should be given a hearing. And that is exactly what he did during the interview.   He asked respectful questions, laid groundwork for Glen's explanations and listened with kindly attention. Glen's time in the closet, with the Bible and *Science and Heath*—getting to know God better—had been well spent. It was literally who he knew that saved the day and that interview.

It's interesting that the intuition to be at the radio station early was acted upon. And it's more than interesting that many objections made in earlier years to the discovery of Christian Science are today becoming focal points of investigation in world thinking. The medical faculty is incorporating prayer into their treatment of patients. The belief in a corporeal God is giving way to an incorporeal idea of God, to the provable Principle, divine Love, which loves and heals us. Many churches are holding healing services and as it's no longer unusual for a woman to write on theological subjects, pastors are placing *Science and Health* into their own libraries and using it as a reference book for their sermons.

Moreover, modern scientists can hardly object to Mary Baker Eddy's slim sense of matter as they themselves are now peering into, and discovering, the insubstantial nature of it. Spirituality is on the rise and man's thirst for higher knowledge will be rewarded. The quiet questions will be answered.

Even when there's no answer, There Is An Answer

Our divine Parent is Love itself and if we could understand this divine Love and its infinite ability to care for all of creation—including the beloved spiritual ideas that it has formed, its sons and daughters—then we would surely never lack for anything needed. Jesus explained that if we as human parents know how to give good things to our children how much more is our Father in heaven willing and able to care for us. He urged us, "Ask, and it shall be given you . . ." (Matthew 7:7).

Not in our best interests.

So why don't we always receive what we pray for even when we believe we will? There may be a few good reasons for this. One is the area just discussed: the need to understand God better. But there's more to it and *Science and Health* (p. 10) tackles this point. "The Scriptures say: 'Ye ask, and receive not, because ye ask amiss, that ye may consume it upon your lusts.' That which we desire and for which we ask, it is not always best for us to receive. In this case infinite Love will not grant the request."

When we think about it, why would our heavenly Parent fulfill a wish list that's not in our best interests? Even a good human parent wouldn't do that, as the following shows.

A very energetic and rather strong little boy, of about two years of age, suddenly appeared with a double-edged razor blade clutched in his pudgy little fist. The young mother didn't have time to wonder where and how he got it but immediately demanded that he hand it over, to which he stoutly replied, "No!"

Again, she firmly directed him to loosen his grip and again he refused to let go of his bright and shiny plaything. His mother had no alternative but to grasp his wrist in one hand and with her other hand pry his fingers off the razor blade. Fortunately, it fell to the floor without harming either of them. But the child, so sure he had been unjustly deprived of his new toy, turned a few shades of purple as he let out wails of displeasure. Regardless of his misery, his mother knew it was in his best interests.

How many times do we hold on to our razor blades, insisting that they will give us pleasure if only we could keep them! All hurtful habits, wrong relationships and ignorant attempts at joy fall into the razor-blade category. Our heavenly Parent is all the while telling us to drop it, to let it go for something of lasting joy and substance.

If we "ask amiss," for wrong things, we should be grateful not to receive them. We can't mistake our desires for God's plan. I remember urging a woman to ask God what His will for her was. She replied, with genuine surprise, that she thought that what she wanted *was* what God wanted.

A little girl I heard of knew better. She very much hoped to have a horse and even prayed for it. But when the horse was not forthcoming, she was teased by friends who said that God had not answered her prayer. She replied, "Oh, yes, He did. God said 'no.'" She knew that "no" was an answer. But how like human nature to assume that only a "yes" to our desires constitutes answered prayer and that somehow there is a breakdown in communication (not our fault, of course) if a "yes" does not appear promptly or at all.

As Glen would often say "we can't plan good enough." No, this was not an attempt at ungrammatical humor, though Glen was well capable of it (the humor, not the lack of grammar). In that sentence "good" is a noun. We don't know enough about what is truly good to acquaint God with the perfect plan for us. But we can ask to see God's plan and then trust the divine Mind to reveal it to us. Our plans, our designs, need to be divinely reviewed and usually amended.

Some years ago I was preparing the illustrated book *Bird* for publication. My artist was a few states away and so to confer about the drawings both he and I bought fax machines. There were a few photographs of the little house which figured in the story and the artist used those with input from me. Other ideas for which I had no example, I'd simply sketch out and then fax to him. I've joked that my fax was like a magic machine. I would feed it crude drawings and sketches and back would come beautifully illustrated works of art. Quite impressive! (If a cave-dweller had seen this procedure he might have ascribed it to some unseen deity.)

This is actually what should happen with our designs, for we can't "plan good enough." We need to "send," take our desires to God and not be surprised if they come back spiritually refined, perhaps quite different but better than we could have imagined. The very first page of the chapter "Prayer" in *Science and Health* contains this statement, "Desire is prayer; and no loss can occur from trusting God with our desires, that they may be moulded and exalted before they take form in words and in deeds." We can and must trust the great architect with our hopes just as I trusted my artist at the other end of the fax machine.

By the way, the cover of this book is one of the drawings from *Bird*. It shows the little house in which many spiritual lessons were learned. For now though I'd like to talk about a different house, one that you and I may have in common.

The house on Kangaroo Street.

Strange as it may sound, each of us has probably owned a house on Kangaroo Street at one time or another. Let me explain. My family lived in Sydney, Australia, as I was growing up. My maternal grandmother was ushered into Christian Science by the following healing. Being told by a kindly medical doctor that she would need to undergo an operation for the removal of a tumor, Nana instead opted to employ a practitioner of Christian Science. Having received spiritual treatment for the condition, the tumor simply passed naturally from her body and she was healed. My mother was then enrolled in the Christian Science Sunday School.

Now years later my grandparents, Nana and Pop, very much wanted to buy a home of their own. They lived in a small rented apartment where the family usually congregated for a wonderful Sunday dinner prepared by Nana in a postage-stamp sized kitchen. But Nana and Pop had their eyes on the North Shore of Sydney. They found a house to their liking, a house on Kangaroo Street, and purchased it.

However, there were renters in this house and a law was in place at that time barring owners from requiring renters to leave. And these renters were not willing to move. Being a child, the details were not totally clear to me, but I do remember Nana was not able to occupy the home of her dreams. My grandparents ended up selling the house on Kangaroo Street.

Yes, most of us have had a house on Kangaroo Street. We've yearned for a certain place or thing, a certain person, a certain job and not been able to see our yearnings fulfilled. But does this have to be the end of joy and new adventures? Not if we keep listening for the way to go. Perhaps in Robert Frost's words it will be the road "less traveled"—the one that will make "all the difference."

Divine Love's plan is always in place, but not necessarily in the direction we have outlined. This is not a type of fatalism, a call to accept whatever is "dished out" to us, so to speak, because evil is not in God's plan. He doesn't know it or plan it, for evil is a human error, not a divine one. Pain, sin, disease, lack all need to be challenged as not being "in the plan." Those things are obvious. Not so clear sometimes are our own desires, our hopes. Are they "in the plan" or are they not? That's when we need to keep praying and listening.

In my grandparents' case a new path did open up for them for it wasn't too many years later that my parents, my brother and I all moved from Australia. After a year or two, Nana and Pop followed—even more than once. They returned to Australia for a short time but then traveled back to rejoin the family. On a cargo ship that took on passengers, Nana and Pop dined with the little group at the captain's table and enjoyed seeing the tropical islands at which the ship put into port. They lived for awhile with the family in Holland and then in England.

Though Pop passed on in London, Nana's travels continued and, as the family moved again, she later lived in Minneapolis and in Los Angeles. When you think of the time in which the world opened up to her it was quite marvelous. Here was a woman who had never written a check, who hadn't held a job (she could cook to perfection and had a beautiful singing voice, but couldn't pursue a career as it was frowned upon in that day and age), yet who suddenly became, on very little money, a world citizen.

Contrast that with the mornings Nana arose at five before the children woke up so she could "black the stove." I think this must have been to prevent it from rusting. At seventeen she had helped her mother run a boarding house, cooking three full meals a day. She had firsthand dealings with the Australian aborigines. And in a matter-of-fact manner, she told of how women would wait for their husbands to give them money to buy Christmas gifts—and this on Christmas Eve! The husbands too worked long hours. Pop, a kind and patiently hard-working man, always put in a six-day week.

So you can see the house on Kangaroo Street would have seemed to be only just recompense for someone like Nana but the world was waiting for her and she flew to meet it. And all through the years, I never recall her mentioning again the house on Kangaroo Street. By the time she quietly left this experience in her ninety-sixth year in my California home in 1976, she had not only traveled widely and lived in different countries of the world but had witnessed on television the landing on the moon.

I have to add something about Nana and that was her unselfish sense of service to others. Always ready to cook or iron, to babysit the children, feed or care for a neighbor, nothing was too hard or too much trouble. No wonder Nana saw far beyond the house on Kangaroo Street!

A good purpose.

So, can we ever expect to have what we wish for? "No," if it's harmful to ourselves or others, or "not yet" if there is another plan in the wings. "Yes," if it's an honest or good endeavor. Many years ago a teenage girl asked me about her desire for travel. She wanted to go somewhere, see different places but—given her circumstances—that didn't seem possible. There didn't appear to be any way for her hopes to be realized.

I recall telling her there was nothing wrong with her longing to see other parts of the country, or the world for that matter, but I also urged her to think about traveling with a purpose, rather than entertaining a mere wanderlust. She said she would think about that aspect. It wasn't too long after this conversation that the young woman joined the debate team in her college and guess what! They traveled! She accomplished her desire for travel and had a good purpose in doing it.

Sometimes we just have to go forward.

Recently, I noticed a new car in the parking place of one of my neighbors and then saw her outside with a puppy she had just acquired. She was absolutely glowing and even looked like a different woman. Up to this point my neighbor had often voiced her disappointment at apartment living and had felt deprived of her home and garden. She yearned for a completely different way of life.

Now, however, my neighbor had a shining face and joy in her conversation. I asked what brought about the change. She said that she suddenly realized that her life was just slipping past her. She had deprived herself of simple joys and even necessities because the "big plan" wasn't working out. She had, in effect, pushed the pause button in life and nothing was happening at all.

She released this pause button and went ahead with the purchase of the needed new car and the puppy she had so longed for. She was no longer at a standstill. From her joyful appearance, I'd certainly say this woman corresponded with the phrase, "getting a new lease on life."

The story of how the children of Israel had to put their feet in the waters of the river Jordan before it parted for them is a good lesson (Joshua 3). They had to go forward! I've often read of wonderful healings people experienced when willing to do such a simple thing as make the bed. Willingness to go ahead with what one needs to do in the face of adversity requires trust in good. But we're not advancing towards an unknown because the quiet answer we need is always waiting for us. God's goodness is never in question so we are not testing that. No, more properly it is we who are being tested.

One day as I prepared to leave for a morning of college classes, my little daughter was coming down with a cold. Her older brother was in school but the little one went to a nursery on the way to the college. I knew they wouldn't take her with cold symptoms but I went ahead trusting that my prayers would be answered and she would be fine by the time we got there. The children had often experienced quick healings and I had no doubt in this case that the spiritual truths as to her wholeness as God's own child would be effective.

However, upon arriving, she was plainly not quite up to the standard of admission. I was still applying these truths to the situation as we continued towards my school campus. Though I had no idea how this would all work out, it seemed right to go ahead. I had three classes that morning but the second period was the crucial class where an important exam would take place.

My first thought was to go to the college office as a woman I knew slightly from church worked there. I asked if she had any free time to babysit the child for me. She said she wasn't able to do that so I proceeded to the first class, which was now in session. Holding my daughter, I slid as quietly as possible into a seat in the back of the room. Then I requested permission to ask some of my friends in that class if they could babysit during the next period. They couldn't help me out either. It appeared that my upcoming exam would take place without me.

As I listened for answers, the idea came to me to return some library books. While the class continued, I took the child by the hand and we made our way across the deserted campus. It was rather misty that morning and suddenly, out of the mistiness, a figure appeared just before we reached the library. Apart from my daughter and myself this was the only other person in the open area. It turned out to be my English professor for the third period of the day. She asked what I was doing and I told her about my predicament. She looked at me so compassionately and said she was a mother too. Then she invited my little girl to go to her office with her while I attended my class.

After taking the exam, I picked up the child in the professor's office. It was so warm and cozy there and my daughter was evidently having a wonderful time with colored pens, for she loved to draw. As I left with much gratitude, my professor smiled and said, "It's okay about my class next period. I know why you won't be there."

The test I took outside the classroom on that day (the trust-in-God test) had a far greater impact on my life than the exam I took inside. I can't even recall what that one was about! The lessons from going ahead when there appeared to be no solution, no answer to the problem have been long lasting. I still use them today. Interestingly, the woman in the college office later said she could have easily helped me and should have. But, in a way, I'm grateful she didn't. That might not have given me the opportunity to see how God provides the answers. The child was doubtless happier in the professor's office than elsewhere for she was loved and warmed. Going home it was obvious her healing was underway and the cold quickly disappeared.

Perhaps the most important lesson in this was that we do not need to depend on people we know for our answers. Sometimes the very ones we expect to aid us are not the ones to do it. This is not personal. It's between God and us and always has been and always will be! Jesus had to prove this in the Garden of Gethsemane when he asked his disciples to watch with him for one hour and they promptly fell asleep.

If we are tempted to feel let down, betrayed in any way because others (even those for whom we have done much) don't come forward and help us, perhaps for only one hour, then it's helpful to think of this as merely a little Gethsemane experience. Small Gethsemanes can add up to large victories if we are able to maintain our peace and love. Part of the definition of Gethsemane in *Science and Health* (p. 586) is, ". . . love meeting no response, but still remaining love." When we recall Jesus's sacrifice for the world then the trifles we often endure in life have to seem minuscule.

The love we express will always have at least one result that we can never be deprived of; it will enrich our own characters. So, we can be grateful for any little Gethsemane because, after all, Gethsemane was on the road to the ascension.

Removing the fear roadblock.

Speaking of roads, there often appear to be obstacles along the way. It's difficult to make progress on our journey or hear an answer with something obstructing our path. Isaiah the prophet knew that and was intent on removing the roadblocks. He urged, "Go through, go through the gates; prepare ye the way of the people; cast up, cast up the highway; gather out the stones; lift up a standard for the people" (Isaiah 62:10).

One of the most common and persistent stones seems to be that of fear. You have to keep tossing it off the roadway. Let's dispose first of the worst fears, usually to do with an event that never comes to pass. Among some memorable quotes, I have a few lines ascribed to Emerson.

> Some of your hurts you have cured,
> And the sharpest you still have survived,
> But what torments of grief you endured
> From evils which never arrived.

Contemplating various scenarios as to why someone is late, for example, is like writing a scene in a play. We're tempted to write the most horrific ending possible and shock ourselves. How useless is that! Recognizing the nature of the temptation, and that this is an illusion we are helping to create, shows how to eliminate this tendency. Let's not pick up the pen or turn on the computer!

Removing the fear factor is one of the most important things we can do for our spiritual progress, our happiness, and our health. The interesting thing is that fear is truly a nonentity—a type of darkness that light dispels. Fear is simply seeing threatening shapes in the shadows. The answer is always to turn on the light!

Because fear has no real basis for being or identity of its own, it will masquerade under many names which appear to have more validity. For instance, fear may assume the "glass-half-empty" identity. An individual who looks at the world, the government and their fellow beings with suspicion and the expectation of wrong-doing has that "half-empty" attitude, opposed to the one who looks on the brighter side of the "half-full" glass. If the "half-empty" individual makes a good suggestion, others are likely to resist the idea because they can intuitively feel the wrong standpoint. Whereas they may accept the same suggestion from someone without that fear base. The remedy? Turn on the light! In this case, trust in God, not people, and the recognition of present good take out that roadblock.

A constant check on our attitude is a great help. It's like watching the gas gauge in the car or checking our compass bearings. Are we full of the right spirit and are we going in the right direction? The attitude of gratitude is a potent fear remover on our spiritual journey. There is always something for which to be grateful.

I remember reading an account of a woman who was living in her car and who called a Christian Scientist to give her spiritual aid. She was advised to make a little gratitude list. The woman wrote that she was so angry at the suggestion that she hung up on the other individual. But as she thought more about it, she decided to comply. The woman didn't stop at a short list but went on and on. By the time she reached a hundred or so items on her list, she had found a job and living quarters. She was out of her car except for its normal use.

It is not an unrealistic or "Polyanna" attitude to look for and acknowledge the symbols of good around us. When my parents moved to a new country with many demands on their funds, my mother said she gave gratitude for the cars she saw on the road though at that time they lacked transportation. She said that those cars were a symbol of God's provision for His children and she acknowledged that provision, and was grateful for it. It wasn't long before my parents had their needed car.

The temptation is to feel envy, not gratitude, at the sight of another's need being filled. Envy is one of the masks that fear puts on. Greed falls into that category too. But as we turn on the light of gratitude and rejoice over the good that comes to others, we are actually opening up the way for it to come to us too. Good is always present and we just have to acknowledge it and be grateful for it, wherever it may appear.

Surely, one of the worst forms that fear can take is the fear for loved ones. Mother love seems particularly susceptible to this attack. It should be the most immune because mother love is usually the most pure and constant form of love to be found. (This cannot be confused with "smother love" which is possessive fear.) In this instance, parents need to turn on the light to comfort themselves as they have often done for their children. They can be comforted by the fact that God is the only true Parent and that this divine Love is caring for all its children all the time.

God never fears for His children. The light of divine Love does not contain the shadow, or darkness, called fear. That's why John the disciple could say: "There is no fear in love; but perfect love casteth out fear: because fear hath torment. He that feareth is not made perfect in love" (1 John 4:18).

Fear is like a wrong delivery coming to our door of thinking. We have the right to refuse it and to let in calm trust, faith in God, and love for all that is good. Fear is a devilish suggestion and certainly warrants the advice that James gives (4:7,8): " . . . Resist the devil, and he will flee from you. Draw nigh to God, and he will draw nigh to you."

That's how I handled sudden fear one night when one of my children was very feverish. I refused the wrong delivery that was knocking at the door of my thinking, without trying to inspect it or mull it over. It did flee from me rather quickly as I drew closer to God. The child was also quickly healed. We can't inspect darkness, but we can turn on the light!

The basic antidote to fear is divine Love and there are many ways to let Love govern us each day. Gratitude is one way and entertaining loving motives and aims is another. Divine Love is a standard we can raise for the people, so that fear will no longer factor into our life equations. Then we can fill our waiting times with patient trust and with steadfast love.

Sometimes we just have to wait.

Some events logically need a little patience, such as waiting for a baby to arrive. During the pioneer days of Australia, a woman in my grandmother's family hired someone to help her with the heavy household work because she was expecting a baby.

However, as months went by, it became patently plain this was a mistake and she was not expecting after all. The helper was released.

Yes, one thing is certain: what we are—or are not—waiting for does become apparent. It takes patience to allow for the timely emergence of a new event in our lives. But this period doesn't have to be stagnant. It can be full of joy and expectancy of good. No need to feel confined to the "penalty box" of life when it is simply a normal half-time break in the game.

But what if the whole game plan seems to be one long penalty session? A woman I know appeared to have every reason to feel penalized by the good work she was involved with in a philanthropic organization. She worked more than twice the normal hours but was paid for a regular week. Her commuting was hard on her and the family, as was her overtime. But she'd come from a military background and that added to the philanthropic work made her feel as though it was her duty to stay.

She kept on to the best of her ability and continued to pray about the situation. Then right before she was due to leave town to help a relative, a former employer suggested she call a man who needed an employee. At the last moment she did this—explaining she would be away for three weeks. As it turned out he was also going to be out of town for that time (though interviews would be held in the meantime).

On the woman's return, two things happened. The new company still wanted to interview her and her own company let her go—saying they were reorganizing. She explained this to the woman interviewing, who immediately remarked, "Oh, and life has just put this job out here for you." And a perfect job it was! Gone was the long commute (the new company was only three minutes from her home). She could take her lunch to the beach only a block away and she was also permitted to take time off for her children's events. It was a very flexible company. After a few years of what seemed like arduous labor, she was now in her dream job!

Just why are we holding onto a certain job or line of endeavor? is a good question. Patiently waiting on God is quite different from enduring a trying situation out of false loyalty, fear of change, or the belief that somehow God wants us to be there and experience it. Perhaps it was my friend's obligatory sense of duty that kept her locked into that job, but it was certainly prayer that lifted her out of it.

This friend, like many others in a similar situation, was convinced that she had to stay in that difficult circumstance until it improved. She thought that would be her answer. Over the years, I've heard many others make the same comment saying, "I have to work this out right where I am!" Interestingly, it was the morning this woman was working and getting ready to leave town, that it came to her strongly that the situation was not right for her. She did not have to continue in it! Even then she released it to God and was willing to do whatever He would have her do.

It was not two hours later that a man she had worked for five years previously called to tell her husband that a friend of his needed a bookkeeper. He even called back a couple of times to be sure that my friend would indeed put in the call to this other employer. This woman basically took the trap off herself and made way for another answer to enter the scene. As she did, that answer came very quickly.

It's very important to realize that where we are is actually a mental, not a physical, location. It's not a matter of confining ourselves to a certain place and calling that God's will. We do need to work it out where we are—in the quiet place of thought.

That means taking the spiritual pathway out of the problem. So, it's not a matter of either running away or doggedly staying.

The spiritual solution might require the humility of remaining in a situation, but, on the other hand, it might require the courage to leave. Because our loyalty needs to be directed towards our heavenly Principle, which is divine Love, we can refuse the unwise martyrdom of holding onto anything that is not pure, good, or loving. Allowing for a better, higher answer is always the wiser way.

If we have removed our self-imposed traps, and the answer still seems slow in coming, then "Be still, and know that I am God" (Psalm 46:10) is exactly what is needed. Divine Love is still communicating, even as the sun still shines above the clouds, and angel messages comfort us, telling us what we need to know.

In *Science and Health* the scientifically-spiritual concept of conversing with God is explained: "The intercommunication is always from God to His idea, man" (p. 284). Intercommunication, being reciprocal, is not a one-way street, but evidently begins with God. If, as John tells us, "We love him (God), because he first loved us" (I John 4:19), then it must also be true that we speak to Him because He first spoke to us.

When circling an airport, waiting for landing clearance, would we imagine the control tower was not communicating with our plane or had decided not to allow us all to get on with our lives? Hardly. We'd doubtless assume this was for our protection. We might even be grateful not to be rerouted to another airport with the need to retrace our steps.

There are many good reasons why answers aren't immediately apparent. As in a jigsaw puzzle, perhaps a connecting piece needs to be located and placed in position first. It might not be the appropriate time for some right endeavor or we might need more preparation, even wisdom, for our next step. The challenge usually is to trust patiently and not allow ourselves to be mesmerized into inactivity or wrong activity.

In one of his parables, Jesus explains how one should expect to receive the Christ by likening a waiting period to a faithful and also an evil servant left in charge of a household. If the lord of the house is slow in coming, the evil servant might not only cease working and providing necessities to the household, but become cruel to his fellow servants and "live it up" by taking part in drunken orgies. When the lord does come, this unfaithful servant will be cut off from any recompense and be classed among the hypocrites. The faithful servant will be found hard at work. Might not Jesus be telling us how to fill our waiting times for the answers we need—to remain alert and ready, and not abandon our spiritual journey and the tasks at hand (Matthew 24:49)?

I was recently stuck in an airplane for a couple of hours. After flying from the West to the East Coast of The United States for the greater part of a day and having made one stop already, our plane took on new passengers at Baltimore which was supposed to be only a twenty-minute layover. But time kept ticking away as the pilot informed us of stormy weather ahead. So we sat on the runway, joined by other planes, waiting, waiting, waiting to take off for Manchester, New Hampshire, only one hour away.

Those of us who had been on the flight from the beginning looked at the enthusiasm of our boisterous new passengers, who appeared to be college students, and smiled weakly at their joy. This wasn't an inconvenience to them at all. They turned around in the aisles, stood up and joked, talking incessantly.

A major basketball game was being played at that very moment and even the captain joined in the good humor by suggesting over the intercom that cell phones could be used to acquaint passengers with the latest scores. That their favorite Boston team was not winning didn't seem to dampen the students' enthusiasm or quiet their exuberance. Yes that plane really "rocked." Just thinking about it makes me smile.

The two hours of waiting passed quickly and soon after attaining altitude we began descending to our destination. The storm had diminished to the point of lightning at a distance and no rerouting was necessary. What did it really matter that it was midnight and not ten o'clock in Manchester! My brother and sister-in-law who met me were quite cheerful and no one that I could see looked in the least unhappy.

A holding pattern doesn't have to be a disaster unless we make it so. In fact, waiting patiently might prevent a disaster in the making, one brought on by an ill-timed course of action. Yes, a holding pattern can be an answer in itself.

To me, the lesson is that joy, felt and shared, does shorten the waiting period and that there's never a better time to live life well and fully than right now. But speaking of life, let's talk about the opposite for a few moments.

Out of sight but not out of Mind.

Death is not what it used to be. Over the last twenty or thirty years its public image has deteriorated considerably. In fact, death appears to be dying out! First of all, it has lost credibility as an actual event and, secondly, longevity has increased. Today, a company may advise its younger workers to prepare for a retirement based on a life expectancy of one hundred and twenty years. Yes, public opinion as to death is changing dramatically.

Recently, when standing in line in the post office the person next to me mentioned that a loved one had passed on. I made some reassuring comment as to life continuing and immediately the stranger replied, "Oh, yes, and I think I know what they're doing right now!" No hesitation at all. That conversation would probably not have taken place a few decades ago. And it was not an isolated incident as I've had similar conversations with other casual acquaintances. Death is more and more being looked upon as a move, a change. In other words, death is not fatal!

Television programs recounting out-of-body experiences as well as the many books written on the subject have gone a long way to support what Jesus showed centuries ago in his resurrection from the grave. Prior to this amazing demonstration of Life over death, he said that no man could take his life from him and that he had power to lay it down and pick it up again (John 10:18). And that's exactly what he did. But how did he do it?

This explanation given in *Science and Health* of how Jesus raised Lazarus, after Lazarus had been in the grave for four days, gives us quite an insight. "Jesus restored Lazarus by the understanding that Lazarus had never died, not by an admission that his body had died and then lived again. Had Jesus believed that Lazarus had lived or died in his body, the Master would have stood on the same plane of belief as those who buried the body, and he could not have resuscitated it" (p.75).

Now it is one thing to believe that someone did not die in their body but quite another to understand that the individual never lived in the body either. You can't move or die out of what you have never lived in. That's logical, but now here comes the really startling part. Jesus showed the relationship of mind and body to be the exact reverse of popular opinion. He proved that the body is in the thinking, not the thinking in the body. That's how he could put the body down and pick it up again.

If one were inside a container then it would be impossible to pick up or put down that container. If one were simply an essence inside the container and this essence escaped, then it would still be impossible to pick up or put down the container. But, if a container were in your or my possession, well, that's a totally different scenario. It could be moved at will.

Now, just because someone passes on, leaving a body behind, that doesn't necessarily signify their thinking has changed, except of course they do find out they are not dead and that sickness or old age didn't kill them. But they still think of themselves with a body so that's what they see. They have a body like the one they had before death as *Science and Health* very clearly states on page 187. So, getting rid of a material body isn't quite that simple after all, is it!

The only viable way out of the illusion that we live in or possess a material body is through spiritual progress. We still have lessons to learn hereafter until all the limited, mortal beliefs we hold about Life, God, die out and the shadowy, material body loses even the appearance of substance and disappears in the light of truth. This is the highest type of molecular disassembly or "Beam me up, Scotty." But here's where we depart from "Star Trek."

The material molecules will not be reassembled elsewhere but totally dissolved by the conscious understanding of Life, which is neither material nor molecular but spiritual and individual.

"And this is life eternal, that they might know thee the only true God, and Jesus Christ, whom thou hast sent" (John 17:3). Here Jesus places eternal life squarely into the category of understanding, of spiritually knowing God and our relationship to Him, a relationship which Jesus came to prove. Old thought patterns will simply disappear and as they do, we'll recognize the spiritual form of life, or life form, that has always, eternally existed. The real you and me!

Speaking of old thought patterns, in former times it was believed that the earth was flat and that if any sailor were brave enough to venture near the ocean's horizon he just might fall off the edge. There still exists a Flat Earth Society today. (I'm not sure what they believe now or if it's simply a group with a sense of humor.) It may not be too far into the future that the globe's inhabitants will look back at our generation and comment, "You know, most of those people still believed in death! Isn't that quaint!" Yes, we will be their Flat Earth Society.

But no one ever falls off the edge of life. When a loved one passes through that change called death, it's helpful to remind ourselves that they are still receiving answers, the answers they need to their life questions. Just because a problem is not solved on this side of the human horizon doesn't mean the solution is unavailable. It still exists and continues in the forever now. Life continues, love continues, talent continues and solving the problem of being continues. So, the individual is not out of school—or graduated—but is in continuing education.

"Out of sight but not out of mind" is so true. If we are able to hold loved ones in mind, think of them in present terms, then we'll have to admit that no one could ever be out of Mind, out of God. The departed can still listen for what divine Mind is telling them and, amazingly, we may even benefit from this. The chapter "Christian Science versus Spiritualism" in *Science and Health* explains that it is not possible to communicate directly with those who have passed from our sight. They are in a different state of consciousness than we are. (And honestly would we really want to drag them back to a prior state of thinking or development? We all have the right to go forward, including those beyond our view.)

Yes, those gone on have a different orientation or state of consciousness. But that's not the end of the story. Something can come from them to us. However, no channeling or human process is involved because there is only one way it may come. It must come to us "in Science" and not outside of it.

That's a little like saying a problem of long division must be solved "within the science of mathematics" not outside of it. Outside of the science of mathematics, numbers would appear chaotic with no meaning. In the same way, life problems need to be solved within the Science of Life not outside of it. Outside of the Science of Life all creation, including man, is mortal and changeable. "Outside of this Science all is mutable; but immortal man, in accord with the divine Principle of his being, God, neither sins, suffers, nor dies" (*Science and Health*, p.202).

Events that are possible within the framework of the Science of Christianity, within the framework of spiritual understanding, are not possible in another context. And it's important to know that "in Science" evil can never be communicated or sent from one person to another. That was how I comforted a man who thought he was receiving evil influences from the departed. Nothing can come from the departed to us because of that different state of consciousness except for *one thing*, and in only *one way*: "In Science, individual good derived from God, the infinite All-in-all, may flow from the departed to mortals; but evil is neither communicable nor scientific" (*Science and Health*, p.72).

The more we understand divine Science and Life which is God, the more likely we'll be to recognize, feel and experience the individual good that flows to us from those who have gone on. No wonder Mary Baker Eddy encourages us, "Life is eternal. We should find this out, and begin the demonstration thereof" (*Science and Health*, p.246). And what better way to begin than with the two great loves of our lives.

The Two Great Loves Of Our Lives

Usually a child memorizing its "a, b, c's" is quite unaware at first that it is learning an alphabet which is the basis of written and verbal communication. The full impact of that isn't obvious until much later. Over the years, I've become increasingly aware that the life answers we need are firmly rooted in and founded upon the first and second loves of our lives. No, this has nothing at all to do with our first or second childhood sweethearts. This is a totally different kind of love. The two loves are simply the love for God and the love for our brother man.

Earthly classrooms.

Our spiritual lessons in this earthly school begin immediately and each day is full of opportunities to take classes in these first and second loves. We early learn spiritual lessons in the crib and in nursery school. However, even as a young mother with two small children, I didn't fully realize those two great loves were actually the foundational lessons I was learning. Now that I do recognize this fact, I'd like to turn back the clock to the mid-1960s, and revisit some of my spiritual classrooms with you.

The first love.

Combining college with home and motherhood was not always easy. Added to that was the fact that people were calling on me for spiritual aid for various situations, including health problems. A friend recently reminded me that when she'd asked how I studied for school I had replied, "through my daughter's hair," because I sometimes had the younger child on my lap.

So, when our English professor handed the class a meaty assignment—to reply in correct sonnet form and line by line to a sonnet of our choosing—I was not particularly thrilled. Those fourteen precise, demanding little lines! Who wrote sonnets anymore? I certainly didn't. However, now and then I might pen a poem for a special occasion or as the mood struck me. So you can see, in my case, he was not talking to a seriously dedicated poetry writer. Driving off campus that day, I was certainly listening and praying for good ideas.

On arriving home, I obediently sat down with pen in hand and expected an answer—but not just any answer. Somehow I knew it was going to veer towards the subject that most interested me — the spiritual truths I had learned and loved from childhood on up. And so it did! In about twenty minutes there on the page in front of me was the line-by-line answer to the Shakespeare sonnet I had chosen.

Perhaps you can imagine my surprise, gratitude and delight—and won't mind if I share the outcome with you as it helps support the point being made regarding our first love. (And sorry, but this is one instance where I can't undo the formality and make it more casual.)

TWO GREAT LOVES

Shakespeare's Sonnet 18

Shall I compare thee to a summer's day?
Thou art more lovely and more temperate:
Rough winds do shake the darling buds of May,
And summer's lease hath all too short a date:
Sometime too hot the eye of heaven shines,
And often is his gold complexion dimm'd;
And every fair from fair sometime declines,
By chance, or nature's changing course untrimm'd;
But thy eternal summer shall not fade,
Nor lose possession of that fair thou ow'st;
Nor shall death brag though wander'st in his shade,
When in eternal lines to time thou grow'st:
So long as men can breathe, or eyes can see,
So long lives this, and this gives life to thee.

Dear Mr. Shakespeare,

Yes, do compare me to a summer's day,
Though it may some inclemencies entail,
Though perversities bend its infant sway,
Yet budding blooms are not therefore made frail:
If perchance celestial views grow dim
And seem not long their beauty to retain,
To name it nature's cause would be a sin,
When men from their eye-scales will not refrain.
Truly is my eternal summer bright,
No mortal mischief aught from me can take,
Nor is there power in death's fleeting night,
Impossible to die for Adam's sake.
The Father's kingdom is eternity,
This long I live, for He gives life to me.

Close on the heels of my gratitude came the thought that the professor, whose religious leaning was known to the class, might not agree with the concepts involved in the poem. However, that didn't seem truly important. When a spiritual gift is put in your lap you don't stop to wonder how it is going to be graded. So with joy I handed in my assignment.

The second love.

This second experience actually took place before the one just recounted but spiritual order takes precedence over chronological order.

A couple of years earlier, our little family had moved to Los Angeles and had not brought very much with us. For instance, we needed a stroller for our infant daughter. One morning, right after moving in, I suddenly realized we were out of milk and the baby would soon be waking up. Then came a pause in vacuuming to survey the options. Not having a car available during the daytime, I figured I would have to take my four-year old son by the hand and, with the baby in my arms, walk in what I considered to be the general direction of the nearest store. That didn't seem like the wisest thing to do.

Oh, there was also another option. My parents had an office about a mile or two away and I could call them to make a run to the grocery store for me. But they were busy doing wonderful work helping people in need of spiritual healing. Disturbing them didn't seem like a great solution either.

Now, I don't recall specifically praying, asking God about this, though obviously I had the question of what to do. For some reason, however, it came to me to finish the vacuuming, which I did. Immediately afterwards there was a knock on the door. I answered it to find a man standing there. He told me he was leaving work early that day and going home as he didn't feel well but wanted to stop by to see if he could sign us up for his milk route before anyone else took us as customers. Out at the curb stood his personal car, not his milk van.

I said I'd be happy to sign up but wished he'd been there earlier on his rounds as we were out of milk. "Oh, just a minute," he replied and went to his car. He returned with seven little sample bottles of milk—four white and three chocolate. Evidently he kept a refrigerated container in his car and of course the little samples were all free! I do remember sending my prayer along with that man as he left, praying that he would feel as freely supplied with health as we had just been with milk.

When you think of what was involved in this experience, it's quite wonderful. If the milkman had knocked a few minutes earlier when I was vacuuming I wouldn't have heard him. Here was the answer coming right to my door. It was free and arrived before the baby awoke. It's worth noting too that during the entire year at that address no one else ever came to solicit us as customers for their milk route.

Though I recounted this incident a number of times and thought about it for many years, it was never quite clear to me what really happened. What did I do? It would be helpful to know. It's almost like a child questioning how it did something right so it could duplicate it (and the results) later on. But nothing came for many years until one day it dawned on me that it wasn't what I had done. It was what I hadn't done! I hadn't disturbed my parents out of respect for the spiritual help they were giving others.

And it's only been obvious to me years later that both instances—the sonnet and the milk—are companions. They illustrate the first and second love of our lives and how learning and practicing these makes the way clear to hear the quiet answers we need. Could it be so simple that the answer to all that is truly meaningful to daily living could hinge on the first and second loves of our lives? Yes, according to what Jesus told a questioner, it could be just that uncomplicated. In the Book of Matthew (22:36-40) it is recounted that a lawyer asked Jesus:

> Master, which is the great commandment in the law? Jesus said unto him, Thou shalt love the Lord thy God with all thy heart, and with all thy soul, and with all thy mind. This is the first and great commandment. And the second is like unto it, Thou shalt love thy neighbour as thyself. On these two commandments hang all the law and the prophets.

On these commandments—on the first and second loves—hang all the moral and spiritual laws and all the prophetic promises of goodness. More good than we can plan, more happiness than we can imagine, more health than all the books on well-being have ever described is available for us all. No wonder

Jesus also told his listeners not to be concerned about their daily needs, their food and their clothing: "But seek ye first the kingdom of God, and his righteousness; and all these things shall be added unto you" (Matthew 6:33). The kingdom of God contains these two loves. It is built upon them. And to build on anything else is to build on sand. Furthermore, these two loves provide both the launching pad and the fuel for our spiritual journey.

Now, to turn away from human needs is not a natural human inclination. Somehow we think needs won't be solved if we do that. It even seems like avoiding the problem. But if we were to find out that changing our focus from the human problem to the divine solution is the most practical thing we could do and the quickest way to find answers, we probably would be more ready to comply.

I didn't avoid the English assignment but it certainly slid into the back seat and was no longer a driving force. Instead, what I had learned of God and His goodness took over and began to steer the project. My love for God was foremost and this love took form as a sonnet. It took away any concern for a good grade. It just spilled out onto the paper. Suddenly it was my first love I was writing about. Everything else faded into the distance. Without really knowing it at the time, I was "seeking first the kingdom of God and his righteousness" and the sonnet was being added to me. Listening for and writing that poem brought me great joy—and it must have pleased the professor too. He gave the poem an A+.

And then there was the second great love. In appreciation for the spiritual healing work that was going on in my parents' offices, I couldn't deprive others of help by interrupting this work. So without a conscious effort I was loving my neighbor as myself. And love was showered on me through seven little bottles of milk!

Was turning away from concern over the assignment and the possibility of a good grade practical? Was continuing to vacuum when the baby needed milk a wise thing to do? Yes, but only because those actions were in accord with the first and second loves of our life. With those in place everything else needed would be there. And they always will!

The perfect combination.

This third experience happened only a few years after the sonnet assignment and as you'll see it actually combined the first and second loves together into one neat little package; well actually, it was more like a tote bag.

At this point I was working full-time in the healing practice of Christian Science. Needing to be available and near my telephone during the day and in the evenings, I didn't take part in many outside activities apart from church. But I felt it was right to do something for the school's PTA and agreed to being Ways and Means Chairman that year.

I would walk to my office just a few blocks away on the main street while the children were in school and it was then the idea of having a certain tote bag for my books occurred to me. These popular tote bags were not only useful but quite attractive, with decorative imitation jewelry on the front. I picked out the color I liked but then noticed the price—$30 as best I can recall—quite a sum of money at that time.

The thought then came that I could just put it on our revolving charge account and let it, well, revolve till I could pay it off. Somehow that didn't ring true. I wanted to do this the right way, but what was the right way? Then I remembered a statement Mary Baker Eddy had made, "The right way wins the right of way, even the way of Truth and Love whereby all our debts are paid, mankind blessed, and God glorified." (*Miscellany* p.232)

Reasoning this out I figured that my revolving charge card purchase would put us into debt, not pay our debts, so it would not bless mankind in the form of my family. I couldn't see how it would glorify God either. So I didn't buy the bag. However, I did do something. I realized the bag represented utility and beauty, qualities I didn't need to buy because they were part of the Christlike nature I was endeavoring to put into practice. I was daily taking those things to the office with me as I wanted to be useful to my brother man and to share the beauty of holiness, of healing, with others. This realization made me so happy I forgot all about the bag. Then came time for the school's big event.

As chairman, I had planned to raise funds for the PTA by having a rummage sale for which many people donated clothing and bric-a-brac. We had different categories and even a boutique section for specialty items. In appreciation for every volunteer, I told them we could all go through the departments before the sale opened and make our own purchases first. As I browsed the tables, without much interest in buying, I walked into the boutique section and found, to my surprise, one of those tote bags, even the color I liked, and it was in perfect condition. I quickly paid the fifty cents for it—in cash, of course!

The purchase was now able to fulfill the conditions of the first and second loves—to love God and man.

But even before the bag appeared,
and even had it **not** appeared,
I was totally satisfied, and to
me that was the real victory.

But am I loved?

The first and second loves have all to do with our love for God and our love for others, so the question often arises, "But am I loved?" Yes, the desire that seems most common to us all is the deep yearning to feel loved, loved by God and by our fellow beings. Over the years, individuals who called for spiritual help would sometimes blurt out that they didn't feel God loved them. And though I'd comfort them as best I could, reassuring them that God is Love, somehow I never felt the perfect answer was at hand.

Then one day a woman called with a problem and added, "I don't feel loved by God." Same story but suddenly I had a different answer, well, actually it was a question. It came to me to ask her if she had ever done anything loving for anyone else. Had she performed a good deed, spoken a kind word or thought a loving thought? Quickly she replied in the affirmative. She certainly had done all those things. Then I asked her where that ability came from. There was no kindness gene running around in the human body that had been located by biologists.

I pointed out what John the beloved disciple said, "We love him (God), because he first loved us" (I John 4:19). The woman and I reasoned together that any love we express, either for God or our fellow beings, has to be because we have first received love. We can't give out what we don't have. We can't deal from an empty bucket. So the very fact she could express love at all meant that she was already feeling love, feeling God's love for her. This made perfect sense to both of us and the answer satisfied us, as it has others since then. So again, it all comes back to loving more. The prayer—the quiet question—as to how to express more Christly love is our needed answer. It truly is a question of love.

I hadn't recalled at the time I spoke with that woman a wonderful statement on the same subject made by Mary Baker

Eddy in a small book, *No and Yes*. Under the heading "Is there no intercessory prayer?" (p. 39) she wrote:

> True prayer is not asking God for love; it is learning to love, and to include all mankind in one affection. Prayer is the utilization of the love wherewith He loves us. Prayer begets an awakened desire to be and do good. It makes new and scientific discoveries of God, of His goodness and power. It shows us more clearly than we saw before, what we already have and are; and most of all, it shows us what God is.

At this point we find our prayers, if filled with love, are coinciding with the answer from divine Love. The more love contained in the quiet question, the more certain we are to hear divine Love's answer to it. In this way, love becomes the question and Love is the answer. (This convergence of question and answer is more fully discussed a little later on.)

The very first sentence in the chapter "Prayer" in *Science and Health* states the three ingredients necessary to the prayer that reforms the sinner and heals the sick. These three focal points have already been discussed in this section. They are: an absolute faith in God, a spiritual understanding of God, and an unselfed love. What material possessions, houses or business deals could compete with healing the sick and helping someone to advance on their spiritual journey? The car license plate frame that reads, "He who dies with the most toys wins," should be rewritten: "He who dies with the most toys will have the most housecleaning to do hereafter." Our spiritual journey requires that we love both now and later, here and hereafter. It can't be completed without it.

What we need will be added to us as promised; it will follow us as a wake follows a boat. But a boat isn't taken out into the river in order to create a wake behind it. If one looks back while steering, watching for those results, the boat will likely go in circles. The boat is launched for a purpose, to go somewhere. The world would distract us, having us float aimlessly through life or in the wrong direction. So, it's imperative to keep in mind the fact that there is a spiritual journey to be made and that all of the world's glamor and glitz is not going to be able to satisfy us if we don't make this journey.

What is truth? was the question Pilate asked Jesus. But an answer wasn't given him because eternal Truth had already been demonstrated. Pilate had missed it altogether. Jesus had a calling, a mission, to present to all mankind the facts of immortal Life, Truth and Love and to live these facts. We all have a similar mission, though it may appear in different forms. Our calling is to love and this calling ensures our progress because love is the pathway that leads home—to divine Life and Love. Home is where the heart is, that's true, and the heart that loves is going home.

Part Two

An Answer We Can Understand

The wonderful thing about quiet answers is that they often appear when you least expect them. The burning question has been relegated to the back burner and you're not sure if it's even simmering. But then the answer (like unexpected joy) comes bubbling to the surface. It's like reaching a plateau on a mountain climb and surveying a breathtaking view. You breathe deeply the fresh air and for a moment contemplate with great gratitude just how far you've come.

However, as you resume the ascent, it is amazing what distance there is yet to travel. Mountain climbing is always like that—the top appears to be just another hill or two away. But of course, there's much encouragement in that. The expectation keeps us going and inspires us to explore vaster regions and higher peaks.

Metaphysics or physics?

There is no mystery to metaphysics if properly understood. However, because the second part of this book delves more deeply into some of the questions discussed earlier, it would be wise to define the parameters of this part of our journey. Metaphysics basically means "after physics." According to *Webster's Dictionary* it was a distinction Aristotle made as to the order of study. Physics—the study of matter—would come first, aided by the senses' observations. Metaphysics would come after this study and is literally "the works after the physical works." So a discussion that is metaphysically based is leaving physical moorings to explore non-physical or mental regions.

Metaphysics was also formerly defined as the "science of the mind"—as opposed to physics, which is defined as a "science that deals with matter and energy and their interactions" (Webster). Lines are being crossed today as forays into the mind/body relationship take place. This uneasy union of metaphysics and physics may trouble some but, to others, may provide a ray of hope for a more enlightened society. At least it appears that mentality is being brought into the human equation, so that man is no longer merely a piece of meat to be inspected. We can be very grateful indeed, for this surely is progress.

However, combining metaphysics and physics actually straddles two standpoints, and, at some juncture, the individual will have to decide for one or the other basis of life—the physical or the metaphysical. Jesus said very decidedly, "It is the spirit that quickeneth; the flesh profiteth nothing . . . ." (John 6:63). In her *Miscellaneous Writings* (p. 170) Mary Baker Eddy pointed out that: "The method of Jesus was purely metaphysical; and no other method is Christian Science."

Of course, this method would not go unchallenged either in Jesus' time or in ours. In choosing the metaphysical basis for life, *Science and Health* contains the chapter "Science of Being" in which the Goliath of "materialistic hypotheses" challenges metaphysics. "In this final struggle for supremacy, semi-metaphysical systems afford no substantial aid to scientific metaphysics, for their arguments are based on the false testimony of the material senses as well as on the facts of Mind" (p. 268).

Most of us can recall the song: "Accentuate the positive, eliminate the negative, latch on to the affirmative and don't mess with Mr. In Between." In this case, the in between is the semi-metaphysical. The song had it right as we can't ride two horses.

One who has advanced sufficiently to plant their feet squarely on the metaphysical basis will need to watch that they are not pulled backwards but maintain their standpoint while encouraging, not condemning, others who are still making that transition. Human thinking must be allowed to advance and sometimes this appears as adopting a dual standpoint for a period of time until one wins out over the other. That upward transition is not adulteration but allowable progress, whereas being pulled backwards to two standpoints would be an adulteration.

Jesus explained where his consciousness actually resided even while it appeared he was physically here on earth. He made this amazing statement: "And no man hath ascended up to heaven, but he that came down from heaven, even the Son of man which is in heaven" (John 3:13). Surely, he was telling us of the spiritual basis from which he worked and thought. He was always on his home base—looking out from this mountaintop view. What Jesus thought and did was beyond or "after physics," so to follow him we will have to go there too.

Our spiritual journey, being metaphysical rather than physical, is not a journey into time and space but a journey into timeless, inner space. Not into the human mind but into the divine Mind which is God, and in this Mind we find beautiful scenes of creation with form, outline, color, diversity, quantity and quality, but with no material limitations. We also find countless ideas—the sons and daughters of God—and they are truly spiritual beings, sublimely happy and totally at peace because they possess the consciousness of harmony which is health. This is our mental, mountaintop view.

The mathematical universe of numbers and their functions is present here and now but many are totally unaware of it until gaining a sense of mathematics. And the spiritual universe is present here and now but most are unaware of it until gaining a sense of Spirit. We need to look past or beyond the material senses in order to see it. We need a different viewing medium—spiritual sense. By accepting the scientific, spiritual facts of being, we have a basis on which to stand and from which to work out the problem of being.

Jesus urged this spiritual standpoint. "Be ye therefore perfect, even as your Father which is in heaven is perfect" (Matthew 5:48). And from *Science and Health* (p. 259): "The Christlike understanding of scientific being and divine healing includes a perfect Principle and idea,—perfect God and perfect man,—as the basis of thought and demonstration."

Understanding home base.

Now, our spiritual journey actually begins mentally at the mountaintop's peak. That's our home base—just as a baseball player comes up to bat at home base not out in left field. The same method is often employed in a mathematics class. Did you ever use a textbook that showed the answer in the back? That math problem began at home base—at the point at which one needed to arrive. It was a known answer (no one was in the dark about it), but steps had to be taken to prove the solution. In much the same way, Christian Science begins with metaphysical, spiritual reality as its home base and our work is to arrive at that correct answer—to understand and experience it—to run the bases.

But what does the chalk—the human scene—on the blackboard tell us? It says we begin out in left field, a term that was adopted from baseball to signify being off base, not on target. From that perspective, the game or purpose changes. So instead of infinity and expansive views of creation, we find limited, murky views of goodness and a horizon over which we are supposed to fall. We're suddenly in a different ballpark. Even the players look a little strange and our relationship to them is often doubtful. Mistakes may be made in recognizing a teammate due to our false viewpoint.

Which view can we trust? What will be our standpoint? If we reply that we'd like the mental mountaintop view—to work out from the standpoint of spiritual reality as home base—then answers will be readily accessible and more meaningful than we can imagine.

Is religion going to play a part?

Like faith, religion is something everyone has in one direction or another. Some may exercise religiously or consume certain foods—even to the point of endowing these activities with supernatural powers. Others bow down to the god of business or money. That's considered normal while those who "get religion" may be viewed as fanatics. However, a thinking man's (or woman's) religion is much to be prized. "For wisdom is better than rubies; and all the things that may be desired are not to be compared to it" (Proverbs 8:11). "Wisdom is the principal thing; therefore get wisdom: and with all thy getting get understanding" (Proverbs 4:7).

Because the discovery of Christian Science enables the Bible to be understood and seen in its divinely scientific, spiritual light, quotations will be given from *Science and Health* in support of various Biblical and metaphysical points. So, it is a matter of religion only in the sense that this spiritual discovery allows for a fuller and more understanding worship of the Supreme Being. Christian Science enables one to put into practice the healing truths contained in the Bible.

Just as the Bible is for everyone, so is the book *Science and Health*. All religions, all spiritual seekers, all physicians, lawyers, economists may freely study and reference these books for their spiritual insight and practicality. Those seeking answers to life's questions will find the path made plainer through this spiritual study and application. The answer is always present. We just need to listen carefully for it. But, in some cases, that is more easily said than done.

What color was the light?

While visiting another country, a girl in her late teens met and dated a kindly honest man who was ten years older. When she returned to the country of her residence, he wrote twice daily with proposals of marriage and after a year came to claim her as his bride. Although having stated she'd welcome him as she would any other friend, in the face of his serious intentions the young woman began to warm to the idea of marriage. (Marriage was a general expectation among young woman in the 1950s who looked forward to a "prince charming" rather than a "career charming.")

While praying about this important decision, she opened her Bible to this verse: "Shall not God search this out? for he knoweth the secrets of the heart" (Psalm 44:21). Not quite sure what that meant, the young woman nevertheless took it as a green light—a go-ahead sign—though her mother had misgivings as to the appropriateness of the marriage. At this point it might be worth mentioning that unless a mother is totally meddlesome, it would be well to listen to a mother's intuition. While not always sure what will make her child blissfully happy, a mother often has an antenna that picks up warning signals.

It was only a week after the quick marriage that the young woman realized there was no real communication—and no meaningful shared interests—between them. She mentioned this to her dad who assured her that she would somehow work it out. Despite any initial doubts, both her parents were supportive of the marriage. As years passed, from time to time the young wife fleetingly considered separation. However, just as quickly she would reject divorce as a solution. Jesus' words, "What God hath joined together let not man put asunder," seemed so emphatic! She also trusted the counsel found in the chapter "Marriage" in *Science and Health*, urging married partners to stay together until there was nothing left to hold onto or until the situation was righted (p. 67).

However, that chapter also included this comforting statement, "From the logic of events we learn that selfishness and impurity alone are fleeting, and that wisdom will ultimately put asunder what she hath not joined together" (p. 60). "Wisdom will put asunder!" How different from divorce where man puts asunder, and how incredibly kind. Wisdom would solve the situation as needed.

It finally became clear to the woman that she had not truly understood the original answer she'd been given. Rather than a green light, that Bible verse was more like an amber light preparing her to stop while the divine Mind revealed to her what was in her heart and what her overriding interests were, and whether these would or would not be compatible with those of her prospective husband. In short, would this couple make good life-traveling companions or teammates? The "wait" answer would have been perfectly clear had she not zeroed in on only "stop" or "go." It's interesting, isn't it, that under pressure to make a decision only a decisive "yes" or "no" seems viable. To wait does not conform to pressure.

The young woman had not really obeyed the answer. She hadn't waited for God "to search this out," but her life was far from empty. She was grateful for the opportunity to attend college (though one male professor in a night class—in which she was making A's—suggested she should be at home washing diapers). The woman also appreciated all the fine qualities of her husband and was busy raising two children, helping other family members, and taking calls from those in need of spiritual assistance. She was too well-employed to dwell for long on her marital situation.

However, as her older child graduated from high school, the woman's marriage suddenly appeared to be in transition. She prayed fervently to have the answer shown her and in plain language that she could not mistake. Opening her Bible, her eyes and fingers fell on these words from the Book of Ruth, "Wherefore she went forth out of the place where she was . . . ." (Ruth 1:7).

And so the marriage came to a close and in a very gentle manner. The woman and her ex-husband still remain on friendly terms including a letter now and then. No one was injured as "wisdom put asunder" what it had not joined.

At the conclusion of "Wedlock" in her *Miscellaneous Writings* Mary Baker Eddy wrote, "Science lifts humanity higher in the scale of harmony, and must ultimately break all bonds that hinder progress" (p. 290). The woman was grateful for all the good the marriage had brought into her life and wouldn't have changed any part of it. She had progressed during those years and in that marriage as far as she possibly could. Her husband was also free—no longer duty-bound to pursue a path in which he was not truly interested.

Only the principals involved in a marriage can know (if willing to face the truth) whether it is a human decision (man that is putting asunder the marriage) or whether it is wisdom (divine intelligence) which is separating what it has not joined. It is fruitless to entertain an opinion on someone else's union. There is no inside track for an observer to run on, there being only two tracks in a marriage. I hope this experience will comfort someone else in a similar situation as it has comforted me, because . . . I was that young woman with the amber-light message.

The obedience question and answer.

In part one of this book, I spoke at some length about a man named Glen. The experiences recounted in that section all happened before I met Glen. In fact, I only heard him lecture once and knew nothing about him up until that point. If someone had told me as I sat listening to a lecture in January of 1976 that I would be married the very next year to the lecturer, I would have considered it too incredible for words, but that's exactly what happened. In 1977 Glen Livezey and I were married and it was—according to one of Glen's grown sons—"a match made in heaven."

Our children were grown and my self-sufficient teenage daughter (who lived with us) would leave in a few years. Soon after the marriage, she wrote an English essay on the person who had most changed her life. In glowing terms she described Glen. Now at the time of our marriage, Glen and I had each spent a decade in the full-time healing practice of Christian Science so we had much in common. Our marriage was an unexpected answer in my life, but this was just the beginning and many more unexpected answers were to come.

It was evident from the beginning that Glen and I had been in love with the spiritual truths taught in the Bible, and made so clear by Christian Science, long before we fell in love with each other. Perhaps that was one reason we "clicked" so quickly and accounted for our long metaphysical conversations. This was a subject we couldn't get enough of, it seemed. But it was also apparent to us that obedience to the divine laws had to be paramount in our lives.

Yes, it became increasingly clear that great care must be exercised in how we handled these precious truths. We thought of

Jesus' obedience in all that he accomplished. In fact, we would sometimes ask ourselves and others too: When it came time for Jesus to be on the cross, where was the safest place he could have been? Was it secluded with friends somewhere or out of the country altogether? The only viable answer we could ever come up with was that the safest place for Jesus to be was on the cross because it was the most obedient. Oh, he agonized about it in the Garden of Gethsemane. It must have been particularly difficult because he was well able to elude his persecutors. Hadn't he already passed through crowds unnoticed and been able to arrive instantly at a destination! Yes, he was spiritually equipped to bypass that whole experience. But he was obedient!

I had grown up in a loving household in which obedience was expected of the children and so that was not a foreign concept; it seemed natural. Soon after the birth of my first child, I read of an unfortunate incident in which a child was not obedient and so coined the saying for my children, "An obedient child is a safe child." My grandmother had told my mother, "Make your children obedient and everyone will love them." And my dad, a man of kind integrity, counseled me about child-rearing, "Never give an order you don't expect to be carried out." Obedience is a wonderful subject and a whole book could be written on it, but suffice it to say that, to Glen and to me, obeying God's Word offered loving safety and security. But this obedience would require much!

Never trapped!

Decorating our first little condominium together brought us a lot of joy. There was never a dispute over decorating decisions. We had similar tastes and enjoyed exploring the beauties of decorating together in rather the same way we enjoyed exploring the beauties of spirituality together. And unanimity still prevailed when reaching the conclusion that a rather large mistake had been made with the kitchen. Our wallpaper hanger had executed his job admirably—cutting and matching the flowers along the seams of the paper. And without complaint, he'd hung himself almost upside down while papering the ceiling. The window blind, specially made from the same paper, completed this garden effect. We certainly had enough flower power to make a hippie envious! But, as the kitchen was completed, we faced each other with sad expressions. We just didn't like it!

As we had neither superfluous sums of money to fritter away nor a "throw-away" mentality, it was surprising when Glen simply and quickly stated our option: "We'll sleep on it tonight, and if we don't like it in the morning, off it all comes!" He took off the trap! Even the prospect of the work involved in ripping it all out didn't deprive us of a good night's rest. So in the morning, quite cheerfully we surveyed the scene of our possible wall-paper crime and were amazed. "I love it!" "I just love it!" How incredible! What caused the turnaround? With the trap off, we had the freedom to reassess what we had done and with that came the ability to see our different decorating (neither of us had ever had anything quite like this before) in a new light.

Of course, this discussion really isn't about wallpaper at all, but it has everything to do with finding answers. It's very difficult to assess any situation from a trapped perspective (it's the "out-in-left-field" viewpoint). It clouds judgment and won't permit the answer we need to enter. We've already decided we're in a room without a door. When people complain they feel trapped in a certain job, I sometimes suggest that they simply view the job as a temporary position gained through a "temp" agency. Suddenly, the trap is off and the job is seen in a completely different light. When you think about it, even a thirty-year job is a temporary position. We don't know what is around the corner in the next month or year, but we are far more likely to enjoy where we are now and be open to new opportunities by accepting freedom instead of a trap.

No one demonstrated more freedom than Jesus of Nazareth and no one had more obstacles thrown in their path. But the sea couldn't swallow him as he walked on it and walls couldn't contain him as he passed through them. The value of time was totally discounted when he arrived instantly at a destination. Not even the grave had power over him. And he promised us, "And ye shall know the truth, and the truth shall make you free" (John 8:32).

The truth of man's real being as a child of God meant a totally different inheritance from the one the world promises: some poverty, some riches, some joy, some sorrow on the road to a black box in the ground. Our spiritual journey takes us in the opposite direction to spiritual freedom and the understanding of eternal Life—to our heavenly heritage, one that has been here all along waiting for us to claim it.

Paul, after his U-turn, found new spiritual freedom and at the same time had to undergo some of the persecution he had formerly inflicted on others. It seems Paul was either in prison, in chains, or in disrepute and yet this amazing man evidently didn't believe in any type of trap, either for himself or others, because this is what he wrote to the Corinthians, "There hath no temptation taken you but such as is common to man: but God is faithful, who will not suffer you to be tempted above that ye are able; but will with the temptation also make a way to escape, that ye may be able to bear it" (I Corinthians 10:13).

Right where the temptation, or trying experience seems to exist, right in that spot sits an answer, a way out. And it's not really crucial how we arrived there—whether we ourselves, another individual or a collective decision has brought us to a certain place in our lives. There's still no trap. Even precedence, "the way it's always been done," is not heavenly cement, so it's helpful to begin with the recognition, "I'm not trapped. Divine Love has an answer and I'm going to pray and listen for it." Truly, no one is ever trapped!

Only 2 percent off!

When Glen and I bought a home on a ridge, overlooking a valley, another valuable lesson was learned. Rocks and manzanita bushes filled our eight acres, that curved over the hillside and ran down towards the valley below. A few homes to our left had similar lot sizes but their acreage was planted in avocado trees (which thrive on slopes). Our next-door neighbor told us that his neighbor had informed him that the marker for the property line between their land was one foot off—to his disadvantage. So, he drew up his own plans of where the new line should be and it ran down over the hill, ending up as a triangle which took away ninety of our neighbor's trees. Our friend said that one foot would have been all right but ninety trees was a bit much to deed over to what he considered to be an encroaching inaccuracy, a compounded error.

This whole affair prompted Glen to make the observation that 2 percent off is worse than 20 percent off. The larger the mistake the quicker one is to disagree, but a small error may be overlooked and accepted. Then if one builds on that small mistake it keeps on diverging from the point of truth, whatever that point may be. It could be a geographical error or a metaphysical mistake that might compound. And it may take years before everyone notices the yawning chasm that has been formed and which appears to be recent, though it has been gradually increasing over a period of time. Parties involved in such a dispute often take positions on opposite sides at the base of this wide triangle and become totally polarized when the real need is to backtrack to the source—to the original point of agreement—and settle on where that point is.

Back to our future.

How important these lessons—obedience, not being trapped, and 2 percent off—would become. It was not long after our marriage that Glen and I began discovering some popular views on Christian Science—though well-meaning and sometimes endorsed by those in high positions—were in fact erroneous or off the mark: word meanings had been changed; conclusions reached that were not uniformly consistent with divine Science. Now, if we were simply dealing with a philosophy, it might be only fair and just to give everyone a say in the matter. Each could have a point of view and be respected for it. Or if a recipe were under dispute, every cook would have the right to formulate the quantity and quality of the ingredients. No wrong or right way involved!

But divine Science is neither a philosophy nor a human concoction but the law of God. It is no more possible to "tweak" the divine laws and God's Word than to slightly alter the principle of mathematics. So it was of some concern to us when we realized that words and actions were in effect rewriting the Christian Science textbook *Science and Health with Key to the Scriptures*. If allowed to continue, this would have the effect of making the Science less effective, health precarious, and the key not such a good fit for unlocking the Scriptures.

But who was rewriting this precious discovery? Had someone undertaken to sink the ship? That didn't appear to be true. But we did discover different influences at work. First of all there were strains of teaching—someone's particular brand of unfoldment on the subject. However, a spiritual misstep made by a few individuals could not have created metaphysical mayhem if others had taken the time to verify what was being shared.

There was also a collective influence. Certain scientific terms in the Einstein era, for instance, had been adopted into the language and vocabulary of students of Christian Science, just as physics terms might be commonly used today in this quantum mechanics era. There may be thought-provoking areas of physics that propel one in the direction of metaphysics, but the basis of physics is still material. Regardless of how ethereal that material basis may become, it must finally give place to the spiritual basis of metaphysics. Due to this fact, adopting physics' terminology is risky business.

Lastly, we had to realize that human nature is more inclined to believe than to understand. It seems simpler sometimes to accept an "expert's" opinion on a deep subject than to undertake the work of understanding it for oneself. This is a dangerous tendency when applied to metaphysics, and Mrs. Eddy strongly warned against it. "Nothing is more antagonistic to Christian Science than a blind belief without understanding, for such a belief hides Truth and builds on error" (*Science and Health,* p. 83).

But how did the bouncing ball of incorrect concepts get so far? Was it like one of those large balls in a stadium that the spectators keep sending from person to person? Yes, the answer was pretty simple—people kept it going. The mistakes had become generally accepted. Glen and I came to the conclusion that the basic culprit was the telephone game.

In case you have never played that game; one player whispers a message into the ear of another and the message is passed around. The distortion at the end of the line of players is usually so great that the original message is unrecognizable. Interestingly and unfortunately, it seemed that the metaphysics of Christian Science passed down was distorted, but usually the false concepts or mistakes arrived intact. Perhaps that's a little like gossip. The rumor spreads like wildfire while the truth is mangled. So, we prayed as to how we should approach the problem. Glen even suggested playing the telephone game at one of the all-day talks we each gave yearly to different groups of Christian Scientists. Perhaps that would point up the need to go back to basics, to go back to the books.

One thing was evident. In obedience, we would have to stop playing this game ourselves and check out what we had learned, and every new unfoldment on spiritual subjects, with our textbooks. We suggested to others, "Go back to the books!" "Look up everything on the subject under discussion and don't take a word or sentence here or there and hang a whole theory on it." "Look up dictionary definitions." "Don't fight for a theory; fight for the truth!" And we became accustomed to saying to each other, when a bright new idea hit us, "Just what page is that on? And what is being said consistently on the subject?"

This approach worked well for both the Christian Science textbook *Science and Health* and for the Bible. When a young man tried to persuade us as to a certain view of Jesus we queried him, "If you could ask anyone, past or present, if what you're saying is correct, who would you ask?" We were counting on his reply and he didn't let us down when he answered, "Jesus." So, using the red-letter Bible, where Jesus' sayings are printed in red, we went through the Gospels together. By the time we reached John 10, the young man paused saying there was no real support in what Jesus had said for this theory—a teaching that had been passed down through the ages.

Trust in another, their understanding or their high standing, and our own mental laziness are enough to precipitate the telephone game. "Just tell me what to do or think; don't make me read the directions." Easy to feel that way about the computer! So instructions are passed along on various topics. In fact, that's the basis of heredity. An individual accepts a disease or characteristic, which is passed down until someone else calls a halt to the process and opts out. Going back to the original idea or the original spiritual standpoint of being is always the best advice.

Recently, I made a template from a product that a friend had put out, though I had a number of my own which I could have used. But hers was of stiffer material and more helpful, or so I thought. After production, someone remarked that a common error had been made and a line of print was upside down on just one side of the item. Simple to begin, isn't it! I trusted my friend and her product. Perhaps she had made hers using another's faulty template. The pass-down process has to stop somewhere, not due to lack of respect for an individual's work or achievement but out of respect for the idea itself.

What does all this have to do with hearing the quiet answer we need? Everything! In the proportion that our Principle is misunderstood, the spiritual answer is that much less available to us. Again, this would be true of mathematics if its principle and its rules were misstated. However, to misunderstand our divine Principle would impact more than our day-to-day decisions. It would alter the course of our spiritual journey because the directions for that journey were being changed.

Along those lines, we found this statement in Mary Baker Eddy's writings, "A single mistake in metaphysics, or in ethics, is more fatal than a mistake in physics" (*Miscellaneous Writings,* p. 264). Convinced of the danger, Glen and I forged ahead on our retracing path. We realized that the future would only be safe if we went back and rectified past mistakes. Here was time travel of the utmost importance. There were many pause points along the way—places of rethinking, realigning and new discoveries. However, the details of this travel, and the rigors of our journey, will be omitted except for one branch of the study and practice of Christian Science that heavily impacts the subject of this book.

Our own Mt. St. Helens.

In May of 1980, I was scheduled to address one of the all-day meetings mentioned a few moments ago. Glen would attend as guest of this Seattle group. The members were lively and interested, so we enjoyed our day very much. It was just a weekend visit and as our homebound plane prepared to taxi down the runway, a large movie screen was displaying the TV news of the day, and some news it was! Mt. St. Helens, the local and usually quiet volcano, was in the process of erupting. The pilot, who must have been as intrigued as his passengers, flew around the large mushroom that was forming in the sky, providing us with front-row seats in nature's theater. (It was truly incredible to see it from that angle!)

However, what we were about to "see" the next day moved and startled us even more. It was not unusual (after sharing the good we knew) to find additional joy or insight at our fingertips and this year was no exception. It appears to be a divine law that mandates this effect: Use what you have to benefit others and receive more yourself. Yes, it was only the day after arriving home that Glen made this thoughtful remark, "I don't think we've been making a good enough distinction between prayer and treatment." That short sentence triggered a long journey—one that is still continuing.

Glen was referring to treatment in Christian Science. When patients came to us for spiritual help we gave them Christian Science treatment. This was a mental medicine, applied to their individual case, and consisted of spiritual truths aimed at counteracting the symptoms of the problem or illness in question. During the period from probably the 1950s on up, it was becoming increasingly popular among Christian Scientists to refer to this treatment as simply "praying for the patient."

Obviously, any true practitioner of this Science is going to approach a case with a deep desire to see the patient healed just as a dedicated doctor would approach a patient with his medical treatment. This heartfelt desire is a prayer in itself and is demonstrated in kindness, sincerity, faith and affection. However, a prayerful approach or a prayer uttered on the behalf of someone, cannot be confused with the actual treatment of an individual.

While Christian Scientists or medical practitioners are free to pray for anyone, neither is free to treat a patient without consent, otherwise we would be talking about malpractice. A lawyer may likewise pray for anyone in the courtroom, but is only permitted to argue a case or present a legal defense on the behalf of an individual if employed to do so.

We felt the confusion of the terms, "prayer" and "treatment," had probably arisen from the need to give the public a quick explanation—one that they could readily understand. If asked their profession, a practitioner of Christian Science might simply reply, "I pray for people." That was more understandable than, "I give patients Christian Science treatment." But this blending—the belief that the terms were synonymous—had quite an effect on students of the Science as well as on the public at large. The public were not clear as to the effectiveness and advantages of Christian Science treatment. Practitioners of this Science found their results were becoming more uncertain—not as quick or as decided as before. Students of this Science were also puzzled and wondered which practitioner to ask for help.

As the terms "prayer" and "treatment" became blended in the minds of students of Christian Science, so did the two chapters "Prayer" and "Christian Science Practice," with the result that neither chapter was distinct. Every right or good thought became conveniently catalogued as "prayer," which took the vitality out of mentality. But Christian Science metaphysics is certainly not bland or indistinct. There are many wonderful topics and subjects to be found through careful observation—subjects which fill thinking with endless, interesting diversity.

This was no airy-fairy white cloud of verbiage we were floating on but "mental furniture" that was practical, dynamic, diverse, distinct, beautifully designed and which would support and delight us! Not one detail should be blended or omitted from the design. Now, immediately, after writing this last sentence, I noticed that the word "mental" minus the "n" would read "metal furniture." Oh what a difference a small detail makes: The word, "united" could become its opposite—untied—by the misplacement of only one letter.

This reminds me of a visit Glen and I had with an editor of a religious periodical. She told us that one of her editorials, titled "The Joys of Immortality," had gone through all the checkpoints and almost hit the printing press to go out as "The Joys of Immorality" before someone caught it. You can imagine, she shuddered a little while recounting this.

Remembering how Mary Baker Eddy had prayed, sometimes for weeks, for just the right word in her writings, we realized we couldn't be too careful about the distinction being made in this textbook regarding prayer and treatment.

Prayer and treatment need a question and answer.

So, after Glen's observation we set to work at unraveling the blend, looking closely at the two chapters as they were written. We made lists under the headings, "What prayer is and what prayer isn't" and "What prayer does and what prayer does not do." There was no mention of treatment, patients or practitioners in that first, short chapter, which contained almost ninety references to prayer. On the other hand, there were only three general references to prayer in the whole chapter "Christian Science Practice" (one of the longest chapters in *Science and Health*) which discussed treatment at some length, and included a section "Mental Treatment Illustrated" (p. 410).

It quickly became evident that a mistake of some proportion, like the effect of an erupting volcano, was mushrooming out of control, making muddy trails out of well-defined pathways while stripping fruitage and blossoms from our mental landscape. We were losing the power of both prayer and treatment. This lavalike flow of confused concepts and human opinions was forming a mental overlay over practical truths and so we had to dig to unearth them. As we did, we saw more clearly than ever that a practitioner may pray about a case, and even pray for the patient during treatment, but the prayer itself is not the actual treatment for which the patient needs to give permission.

Just as a physician has been given permission to change a patient's body, a Christian Scientist must have permission before administering the mental medicine or truths which change a patient's thinking and thereby his body.

In a nutshell, prayer is directed to God and treatment to a patient. What a freedom this distinction provided! Gone was the restriction "You can't pray for someone in the hospital." Of course one may *pray* for someone in a hospital, but a Christian Scientist cannot ethically *treat* an individual who has chosen another form of treatment, nor should they treat someone who is under the care of another Christian Scientist.

Suddenly all that Mrs. Eddy said on this subject shifted into focus. For instance this statement, "It is already understood that Christian Scientists will not receive a patient who is under the care of a regular physician, until he has done with the case and different aid is sought. The same courtesy should be observed in the professional intercourse of Christian Science healers with one another" *(Retrospection and Introspection*, p. 87). There is good reason for this professional separation of patients. An ethical doctor would not, in all good conscience, accept a patient already under the care of another physician and administer a totally different medication. One form of treatment might cancel out the other, leaving the patient in a worse state than before.

Now, if a mental medicine sounds a trifle esoteric, let's remember that we take mental doses everyday one way or another to rectify mental mistakes. A true news report cancels out a faulty one. This mental remedy might save us from mental and even physical suffering over something such as a falsely reported death.

Many professionals working in the field of mental illness try to avoid drugs as they treat their patients' mental problems, or when counseling those with eating disorders and other mental maladies. Marriage and career counselors often work with mental remedies by suggesting a new approach in thinking or a character change. With the mental nature of disease becoming more recognized, it soon may not be a giant step to allow the spiritual facts of being—specific mental truths—to be used as an antidote for sickness and disease.

Physical, material remedies are based on the theory of the healing properties of matter while Christian Science metaphysics is based on the healing properties of the divine Mind, on God. At some point it will certainly become more widely known just what is involved in the mental medicine that Christian Science administers. That this medicine emanating from the divine Mind has great potency has been proved in countless lives and is there for the willing inquirer to discover. But let not this inquirer be confused as to what constitutes prayer and what constitutes Christian Science treatment.

This subject requires more space than can be given it in this book on quiet answers but, as there is sufficient interest in the subject, another volume may be undertaken. Suffice it to say at this point, that the thorough exploration of the Bible and of Mary Baker Eddy's writings on the subject produced immediate fruits. For instance, Glen encouraged a worried mother to pray for her grown daughter who had gone into the hospital for an operation but explained she must be careful not to treat her daughter mentally. The mother acknowledged the difference, prayed for her daughter and the next morning the doctors could find no trace of what they had intended to remove.

As we shared these findings from our textbooks with individuals and with groups, we were sometimes met with joy but more often with incredulity, to put it mildly. Many strongly stated that it was unnecessary to ask God for anything as He already knew all. We replied that indeed He did know all and that's why we ask Him. (That was an era when prayer had been overlooked in favor of arguing or affirming spiritual truths, whereas each correct mental approach could have been employed as required.)

Spiritually speaking, we do know the truth for we are the children of God, the reflections of the divine Mind which knows all. However, this fact must be seen humanly. It's the prayer, "Thy will be done in earth, as it is in heaven" (Matthew 6:10). Jesus proclaimed his unity with God in what has been termed his farewell prayer in John 17, and he prayed, desired, that his disciples and those who believed on him through their word would experience this same unity. He prayed that the divine fact of unity, a fact which he forcefully uttered, would be made humanly visible.

Since our own Mt. St. Helens experience in May of 1980, it is far more common to hear other students of this Science asking God in prayer on the basis that God's goodness is already present and available. However, even now in 2003, the distinction as to what Christian Science treatment is and does still lies virtually untouched in writings on healing. I mention this not to create a stir, but to create an interest in the subject, for—if this method of treating disease is to remain intact and continue down through the ages—it will need to be understood.

It will take real courage for those who have practiced or taught Christian Science for many years or decades to rethink the subject of prayer and treatment. Considering what is at stake, there is much more to lose than a personal reputation. And furthermore, there is something refreshing and liberating in being able to say, "We were wrong." When faced with what appeared to be oncoming disaster, the disciples in the musical *Jesus Christ, Superstar* sang, "Could we start again, please?" Glen and I used to say this to each other as we began again at a very logical place—the first chapter in *Science and Health*: "Prayer."

Loving our neighbor or just kidding ourselves? It's a test.

The Parade Magazine of March 23, 2003 contained the article, "Why Prayer Could Be Good Medicine." This article included the following: "To many physicians, the evidence for the power of prayer is far too compelling to ignore. 'I decided that not using prayer on behalf of my patients was the equivalent of withholding a needed medication or surgical procedure,' says Dr. Larry Dossey, a former internist who is the author of *Healing Words* and *Prayer is Good Medicine.* 'I prayed daily for my patients.'" Clearly, the need for this loving care of patients is becoming increasingly recognized.

As Glen and I better understood the metaphysical distinction between prayer and treatment, we also found many opportunities to share this with others and to put it into practice ourselves. In fact, that's how I came to be standing in a Laundromat taking a test. And what is more, it became clear that I was failing the test.

Before having a washer and dryer installed in our home, I used a local Laundromat. One day I'd taken in a large load and, being the only customer, was enjoying the peace and quiet. Suddenly the stillness was broken when a mother appeared with two small children. The baby in the stroller was crying pitifully and seemed to be sick or, at the least, very uncomfortable. The toddler kept yanking at the stroller which only made the infant cry more. The mother, understandably, was quite distracted as she began her laundry.

A little put out at this invasion, I let my peaceful mode lapse a little but then felt I needed to do something constructive. I had no right to give Christian Science treatment unasked for, so decided I should at least pray for the baby. I began with, "May this child feel Your peace, dear Father and may it . . . ." But suddenly I stopped in the middle of my prayer and realized, "You're not praying for that child; you're the one who wants the peace and quiet!" That's when I knew I was failing the test, the one given in the chapter on "Prayer" in *Science and Health* (p. 9): "The test of all prayer lies in the answer to these questions: Do we love our neighbor better because of this asking?" Do we pursue the old selfishness, satisfied with having prayed for something better, though we give no evidence of the sincerity of our requests by living consistently with our prayer?"

It was quite obvious that I would love not my neighbor, but only myself better "because of this asking." So my prayer was failing the test before it was even finished. Slightly appalled at this revelation, I paused for a long moment and established the basis for prayer, reasoning and affirming that God's allness and everpresent goodness exclude evil of any kind. His children could never for a moment be deprived of the harmony that is rightfully theirs. Then I silently petitioned God again, but with more compassion and a genuine desire to help. "Dear Father, may this child feel the peace and health that are present right here and now. May no material circumstance rob it of any of the good you have provided . . . ."

Suddenly I became aware that all was totally quiet and the child was asleep. Though the toddler pulled at the stroller again and the child wakened momentarily, it immediately went back to sleep and remained that way for the time I was there. I was so grateful for the child's peace and comfort. But if the prayer hadn't passed that test, it surely would have gone no farther than the laundry I was folding.

It also became clear to me later that the test of my prayer was not in the child's reaction. We tend to judge prayer that way, but it's not a correct approach. It was not the child's comfort that tested my prayer, but it was love for my neighbor that was the test.

The prayer and the answer coincide.

"The test of all prayer" statement deserves close attention. It says, not just some, but *all* prayer. That's incredibly revealing for two special reasons. Firstly, it shows that all prayer contains petition, "this asking." Christian Science does not remove the basic meaning of the word "prayer" but maintains the humility of asking and the earnestness of fervent desiring (wordless or spoken). It never leaves one with statements only and no desire.

Secondly, it warns us that whatever our desires may be, whether for more humility, wisdom, solutions to a human situation or world peace, that unless these prayers result in loving our neighbor better they are not valid prayers. They do not pass the test. So it all comes back again to the two great loves of our lives: loving God, good, supremely and: loving our neighbor as ourselves.

That's the test, but what is the trigger? How is it that prayer is answered at all? Does something special initiate a good result? This heavenly promise, articulated by the prophet Isaiah, provides us with a very large clue. "So shall my word be that goeth forth out of my mouth: it shall not return unto me void, but it shall accomplish that which I please, and it shall prosper in the thing whereto I sent it" (Isaiah 55:11). Let's build up to that clue for a moment as this is where love as the question and Love which is the answer coincide.

To love one's neighbor as oneself is a divine idea, according to *Science and Health* (p. 88), so it does not emanate from a human being and no one can lay claim to that idea. It belongs to divinity, to God, to divine Mind. The word "idea" in Christian Science may be used in various ways and the context will reveal its application. In some instances, the word denotes our idea of God, or it may point to God's idea or spiritual man. Or, as in the context above, "idea" may infer a divine plan by which something is carried out.

Loving one's neighbor as oneself is a concept or idea that the divine Mind has formulated as an integral part for the government of its own creation. When this idea or activity takes place on the human scene, divine Mind recognizes the idea as being its own, just as any of us would recognize an idea that we had sent out. Without knowing the details of how it was implemented or even the situation itself, the basic concept we had formulated would still be recognizable to us. We would say, "Oh, that was my idea!"

Though infinite, perfect Mind is not conscious of imperfection, human limitations or problems yet the divine idea or activity is known to this Mind. It is at this recognition point that prayer is answered!   (What God has sent out does not return empty or void.) However, half-baked desires for someone's good are not acknowledged by the divine Mind, nor are selfish or doubting prayers. It is only as the idea returns to God in a pure form, the way in which it was sent out, that it is recognizable to God and therefore fruitful. The divine Mind is seeing—bearing witness to—what it has created and declaring it to be very good.

Not Seeing What's There? Five Clues

We've all had the experience of not seeing what is present. A cordless telephone on a crowded desk becomes invisible and sends the owner on an urgent search. Suddenly there is the telephone, lying on its side, but, because of its position and color, it had virtually gone into hiding. A new perspective was needed.

In the same way, because God is good and God is everpresent, it follows that good is everpresent. We can find this everpresent good, not by a frantic search, but, by having another perspective. The allness of God—the allness of good—followed to a logical conclusion, squeezes out the possibility of the presence of another power called evil. This can and must be proved step by step even as we prove the errorless presence of mathematical additions. The errors in mathematics are actually only the supposed absence of the right answer. The Science of the Bible reveals evil to be only the supposed absence of good.

This is a difficult point for human thinking to accept because it appears to challenge the validity of human existence. Many want to believe in and have an errorless spiritual existence, but only allow for it hereafter. Keeping evil in the picture seems to validate the human condition, with all its woes, and allows it to continue virtually unchecked. The resistance to questioning the human scene (we'd rather just have it fixed than questioned) is due in great part to our acceptance of the material senses. Let's remove the barrier to seeing evil for what it is, or rather, for what it is not.

A question of reality.

Is it possible to change reality? Is human reality truly real? Or is divine reality the actual? In line with the former television show on identity, we might ask the question, "Will the real reality please stand up?"

Part of the dictionary definition of "real" is that which is fixed and permanent. If disease is humanly real—fixed and permanent—why undertake the daunting task of getting rid of it by any method? If disease is spiritually real, would it be possible by any means—material or spiritual—to eradicate or heal a part of God's reality?

Jesus came to do God's will not to oppose it. When Jesus healed both the sick and sinning through spiritual means alone, we must assume he was doing God's will. If such things as Jesus destroyed had been known to God, who is ". . . of purer eyes than to behold evil, and canst not look on iniquity . . . " (Habakkuk 1:12) then they would have been part of God's reality and no one should dare to oppose them.

The human tendency is to ask the divine Being to accept a human view of reality and then to deal with it for us. That would be like asking the principle of mathematics to take note, and rid us, of the troublesome 99 we came up with when multiplying 9 by 10. Clearly, we need to change our view and learn more of the principle of math and the facts which erase the wrong answer—an answer which was never real or viable. In the same way, wouldn't it be better to look at creation from God's perspective and not ask Him to accept ours?

However, to view creation from a divine perspective involves challenging the testimony of the material, physical senses (infinite Spirit does not look at creation through limited, physical eyes). But we're on such friendly terms with the five material senses! They seem to offer a kind of pseudo security, though they tell us that this material world is constantly changing. Why, mountains even emerge or disappear over centuries, yet we still call this testimony valid and real. So apparently we do not adhere, in practice, to the dictionary definition. We do not judge reality by what is fixed and permanent, and instead allow for a sliding scale of reality in order to accommodate the material senses. It's a type of magic trick: "Now you see it, now you don't!" But while we see it, we call it real, though it may disappear the next moment—compliments of the material senses. Somehow mankind tries to adjust to this disappearing act of people, pets and associations we value, in order to maintain the honored status of, and our friendly relationship with, the material senses. But, as the saying goes, "With friends like that, who needs enemies?" It's enough to make even the most ardent supporter of the material senses nervous.

Perhaps the final indignity of the material senses is when they, on occasion, inform us that death is a friend of man, whereas the Bible tells us, "The last enemy that shall be destroyed is death" (I Corinthians 15:26). It would appear that the material senses are actually the friends of lack, sin, sickness and death rather than the friends of humanity. Perhaps we need to choose our friends more carefully.

Of course, it is acknowledged the eyes do fool us in certain instances, and we will even redefine reality on occasion. For instance, a counterfeit bill looks and feels real. All can agree that it is tangibly present to the physical sense of touch. But does that make it real in the context of what it represents? Of course not. When you tell someone that bill is not real they understand you are not inferring it can't be felt, but that it has no lawful, legitimate existence and no gold to back it up. The best you can say about it (in a rather oxymoronic way) is that the bill is a real counterfeit.

Mortal man, being subject to sin, disease and death, is a counterfeit condition of existence and does not give the true idea of God's man, made in His own image and likeness—though we can physically see and touch this counterfeit condition. In this same way, evil—be it sin, disease or death—may be thought of as unreal in a divine sense, though it may be tangible to the human, material senses.

In a nutshell, all that the material senses call real constantly fluctuates and changes. God's kingdom is intact, fixed and permanent, and is here to be discovered. Evil has no part of this divine reality and it has no power with which to dispute the power of the Almighty.

The Book of Job (34:4) urges: "Let us choose to us judgment: let us know among ourselves what is good." And Isaiah (7:15), prophesying of the coming of Jesus, said: "Butter and honey shall he eat, that he may know to refuse the evil, and choose the good." As *Science and Health* explains (p. 480): "If sin, sickness, and death were understood as nothingness, they would disappear. As vapor melts before the sun, so evil would vanish before the reality of good. One must hide the other. How important, then, to choose good as the reality!" Of course, the final word on this is: "And God saw every thing that he had made, and, behold, it was very good" (Genesis 1:31).

Of course, the five material senses—our eyes, ears, touch and so on—object to this, as they usually do. They tell us another story—a poorly-written tale of woe and misery in which evil maintains a prominent if not starring role. However, a little happiness may be interjected into the script now and then if you're lucky enough, smart enough, beautiful enough, rich enough, good enough, or any other reason you may like to insert at this point.

No liars on the witness stand, please!

In the old musical movie *Royal Wedding,* Fred Astaire sang what could hardly be called a love song. "How could you believe me when I said I love you when you know I've been a liar all my life!" It was a comedy routine, of course. Now, the material senses have actually always lied, but somehow we keep expecting them to be faithful—to tell us the truth.

Perhaps we become easy targets of delusion because now and then the material senses tell us exactly what we want to see or hear. They may testify to more health or happiness and, because they do, someone may question: Is the evidence of health and happiness we see false because the material senses lie to us? Is this good report incorrect? No, it is not incorrect. However, it is not because of what the material senses say but because of the spiritual fact that the information is true. The truth is that man, in God's image and likeness, is a spiritual idea and is indeed happy and healthy, right here, right now.

So, if the material senses testify to the fact of health, it's like chalk on the blackboard agreeing with the principle of math and showing a correct solution to a problem. The chalk can be right or wrong but that doesn't change the correct answer in the slightest. It's not because of what chalk writes that we can send up a shout of victory.

That's why Jesus could thank God before he saw the physical evidence of healing or before the loaves and fishes were multiplied. He was giving gratitude for the spiritual reality and the chalk—the human scene—just had to shape up and agree with the divine fact. It's dangerous to rely on the testimony of the senses as to our well-being because they shift like sand. Far better to build on the bedrock of spiritual understanding.

The telephone game.

As I mentioned earlier, Glen and I had discussed the possibility of playing the telephone game at one of the yearly meetings we addressed, and finally I did just that. Nine volunteers came down in front of the audience and stood in a line. The first statement was a simple set of directions to someone's house. The first person read it silently, then whispered it into the ear of the next person and on it went down the line. The ninth volunteer spoke out loud what was said to them and then the first person read the original. Well, there was no way you could have made it to that house with the whispered directions. You'd be absolutely lost!

The next sentence passed on down was something with which the entire group was familiar, but the result was the same. Quite garbled. And so it went with the third message, which was also rather familiar to everyone. Amid much laughter the point was made. One cannot rely on information passed down but must go back to the source. No one had the intention of subverting the truth but it just happened in the pass-down process.

Each of the nine people represented one decade and this gave us a feeling of what might have happened over the last ninety years. Of course, that was really generous. We could have stipulated one person per year which would have made the outcome even worse.

A friend, thinking she might be interested in doing that at a similar talk, asked how I knew they would get it wrong. I told her that it never occurred to me for one moment they would get it right. That's just the nature of the telephone game, otherwise it would be no fun at all to play.

"At the old ball game."

So much for what our ears tell us! But just to play fair we could find out how the eyes shape up in individual cases. We'll bring them up to bat, and see if they do anything to dispel our doubts as to just where and how they are playing this game.

"Play ball!"

Willy's Story.

Years ago a friend named Jane owned a dog called Willy, a cute little dachshund that Jane enjoyed very much. However, he hadn't always been her dog. A friend of hers, let's call her Mrs. B., had previously owned Willy. One day as Mrs. B. was getting ready to go to a party, Willy slipped out the door and ran off. (It might be worth mentioning at this point that Willy was not known for his obedience skills.)

So Mrs. B. hurriedly finished dressing and drove around in her car to look for him. She soon spotted this cute little dachshund sitting serenely on the porch of the house behind hers. She scooped him up, gave him a little swat on the behind as a reprimand for running away, took him home and deposited him in her living room. She then left for the party.

While she was gone, Mrs. B's father (who lived across the street) saw Willy running free in the front yard. It appeared the little escape artist was at it again! Her father went over, collared Willy and put him into her living room. Then he noticed another dog sitting there already. So he called Mrs. B. to inform her that she now had two dachshunds in her living room.

In the rush to retrieve her pooch, Mrs. B. had actually made off with her neighbor's dog. Adding to the humor of this story is the fact that if she had been in less of a hurry she just might have noticed that the dog she had kidnapped (or rather dognapped) was in fact a girl, whereas Willy was a boy.

However, Jane had a winning way with Willy for he was perfectly happy to obey her. That's the story of how Willy came to be Jane's dog. It was a win-win situation for Willy and Jane, but not so for the material senses. That was "Strike one!" The lesson here is that the rush to find a quick answer doesn't put one in a good position to hear the quiet answer. Our eyes might tell us what we want to believe, and they just might be wrong!

Hi, there!

Next let's go to a restaurant in San Diego where friends of mine usually celebrate their anniversary. One son and his family live in the area and he had spoken to his mother just a short time before she and her husband left home on the night in question.

The restaurant had a view of the airport and my friends were watching the planes fly in and out while waiting for their table. Suddenly someone behind my friend put a hand on her shoulder. She thought that was a funny thing for a waiter to do and looked at her husband. He was smiling so she turned around expecting to see a friend who was an airline pilot—but it wasn't the friend. It was a man she didn't recognize.

So again she turned to her husband for clues, but he was still smiling. She looked back at the man again, even more puzzled, and then heard these words, "Mom, don't you recognize your own son?" It was a little dark in there, but even after a third look it still didn't register with her. With that her husband pointed across the room to a table where the whole family was seated. He had secretly invited them to surprise her. And surprise her they did! Her son was the last person she expected to see in that restaurant, so she just couldn't see him. That was "Strike two!"

STRIKE TWO

The unreliable material senses are at it again. No one's fault really. It was simply that the material senses told Mrs. B. someone else's dog was hers because she wanted to believe it. On the other hand, my friend's eyes (her material sense of sight) told her that her son was not present because she couldn't believe it.

Lost and found.

Just for a little variety, let's go to Sydney, Australia, about the year 1917. A woman had taken her small daughter into town with her to do some shopping. After awhile, they became parted in the crowd and the woman searched anxiously for her child. On not finding her, the distraught mother then rushed off to the police station to report that her child was missing.

After the mother had poured out her sad story, the policeman on duty went into another room and, in a moment, returned with the child in tow. The woman, with her eyes still clouded by grief and fear, took one look at her daughter and loudly proclaimed, "That's not my child!"

How long it took my grandmother to recognize my mother I don't know, but the question could be posed: Who was actually lost? The child was found but the child's mother was so lost in grief she literally could not see what she didn't believe to be possible. So, here are these same material senses performing strangely at every turn of the road, all depending on what the individual believes or does not believe. No wonder Mary Baker Eddy wrote in *Science and Health* (p. 86), "Mortal mind sees what it believes as certainly as it believes what it sees."

At this point it might be appropriate to hum the last line of the baseball song, "And it's one, two, three strikes you're out at the old ball game."

The material senses claim to be the only avenues of understanding life. They claim to be accurate witnesses and that their testimony is valid. But let's suppose for a moment there is a reputable newspaper which, after carefully monitoring the game, has strong doubts about the claims of the material senses. So one of their trusted employees, a respectful reporter (R.R.), is sent out to interview the material senses (M.S.) about the game to find out just what went wrong.

The strike-out interview.

R.R. You struck out three times. How do you account for that? Were you off your game or is this normal for you?

M.S. Oh, sometimes testifying can be "iffy"— a hit or miss proposition. That's just part of the game.

R.R. Would you mind explaining?

M.S. Well, in the second strike I simply wasn't ready. The batter was thrown a curve. She didn't expect to see her son, so how could I testify that he was there? And the first strike was miscalled. I found a dachshund for the woman.

R.R. Yes, but it was the wrong dog.

M.S. Details, details. Her anxiety to be on time put me off my game. Not my fault.

R.R. So, what you're saying is that you give people what they expect. So how come you struck out with the child? You didn't give that mother what she expected.

M.S. I gave her *exactly* what she expected. She didn't think the child was found and so that's what I testified to. I told her it was not her child.

R.R. This is very confusing.

M.S. Get used to it. Even confuses me.

R.R. But you do sometimes testify about happier things, don't you?

M.S. Oh sure, if people are determined to dream up something they'd like, I occasionally give it to them. I have no trouble as long as they are in the same ballpark, on the same page as I am, if you know what I mean.

R.R. No, I'm not sure that I do.

M.S. Well, I testify about matter. The material senses, get it? Matter is my basis—my home base. That's why so many events are, eh, well, sort of limited and die out. But as long as people place their hopes and joys on matter, I can testify. It's not my fault if it doesn't hold up.

R.R. Aren't there other things you testify to—things that are good and lasting?

M.S. Oh, ah, yes, there are the mystery events. They are always good, though I don't know where they come from. It's very puzzling to me, but I just go along with it.

R.R. So, do you come with any kind of warranty?

M.S. Don't be ridiculous. I reserve the right to fluctuate, according to what people expect or don't expect. In fact, sometimes I'm even absent. People think they lose their material senses.

R.R. Doesn't that arouse suspicion as to your reliability as a witness, if you can't be counted on to be present?

M.S. Not at all. People love me and rely on me anyway. Besides, what other game is there in town?

R.R. Well, I have heard there is another ga . . . .

M.S. Look, did you hear it from me? No! Besides, all the physical laws depend on my testimony too. I'm very important.

R.R. I heard that Max Planck, the well-known quantum physicist, said that we have no right to assume that any physical laws exist.

M.S. He was a traitor! How can you possibly tell what exists without my expert witnessing?

R.R. Actually, I have heard rumors that there is a spiritual reality and matter plays no part in it.

M.S. That's a vicious lie! Don't listen to it. Look at all the matter in the universe.

R.R. Speaking of that, I have to go now and cover a physicist's convention. They are coming up with some intriguing theories on that subject. Some say the matter of this whole earth can be reduced to a size smaller than a baseball, if you take all the space out of it.

M.S. Just a minute, what was that? Smaller than a baseball?

R.R. Yes, that's what I said.

M.S. Say, um, something just occurred to me. You don't happen to know of a witness protection program do you?

R.R. Sorry, but I don't.

M.S. Smaller than a baseball! I can't comprehend that. I think I'd better go lie down.

R.R. Good idea. May you rest in peace!

Spiritual Sense to the Rescue

Now, let's go to another ballpark for a different game. Let's go to Palomar Mountain about 45 minutes north of Escondido in Southern California. Rising to a height of over 5,000 feet, the mountaintop community claimed only 200 full-time residents at the time Glen and I lived there.

The little house we'd purchased sat on ten acres of beautiful woodland property. Built by two ships' captains, it was absolutely picturesque but hardly a commodious or comfortable dwelling. However, the insulation and woodstove we installed did make it a cozy classroom. A chain-link fence had surrounded the house to keep a horse from wandering all over the acreage, and the basement that became our bedroom had obviously housed a goat and other small creatures. The pump for the well wasn't working, neither was the plumbing. Added to that was the accumulation of thirty years on the acreage itself. We disposed of and also sold off a tremendous assortment of collected items, and fixed the well and the plumbing.

Finally from all of this emerged a lovely little storybook cottage set among tall cedars, pines, firs and even a redwood or two. The long dirt driveway meandered through open fields of fiddlehead ferns towards the house, which was hidden from the roadway behind the majestic trees. It did seem to be an idyllic setting (arrived at through much labor) for our spiritual lessons.

Definitely not a telephone game.

It all began with the telephone but this was definitely not a game. Our bedroom on the lower level of the little house was made out of rock. The closet was enclosed by rocks, the walls were rocks and the pedestals beside the bed were also made of

153

rock. Our telephones—one for each of us—sat on either side of the bed on the rock pedestals. The whole room really did resemble something from the television cartoon *The Flintstones*.

After we were sound asleep one night, a telephone suddenly went off. I say "went off" because it sounded more like an alarm clock than a telephone. This was a little puzzling, especially as there was no one at the other end of the line. But Glen and I were now wide awake and so began to review the previous day with all the spiritual lessons learned. Wonderful new ideas came to us about God and His goodness and insights that we really needed.

This was our first session of "night school" (though it was not so named until a number of nights followed the same pattern). Oh, the telephone didn't buzz again but something else would wake one of us up and suddenly we'd both be awake, listening for and discussing ideas. We didn't turn on the light or get up but remained in a quiet, alert state. And though these night-school sessions could last as long as a couple of hours, we never felt tired the next day.

The subjects under consideration would vary from what one might consider very positive to others that were quite negative, such as pride, impatience or speculation as to others' actions. Then, of course, we would have to put the opposite qualities into practice. It became more obvious that each day of this earthly experience is one big classroom where we learn more of the Principle of all true being and also where we have to let go of the human errors which impede spiritual progress.

We became so eager for our night sessions that if many days went by without a night school we would pray, "Dear Father, please show us our next step," and then night school would take place again.

These classrooms prepared us for answers to the many questions we had. The questions could be quite simple (having to do with daily life) but usually veered towards far more important topics. How could we express more of the Christlike nature? How could we help others better see their God-given freedom? Or it may have been a "mystery" statement in our textbooks, the Bible, or *Science and Health* that puzzled us. Answers began to appear more frequently and with less effort. There were instances, however, when an answer didn't appear.

One day as we made our winding way down the mountainside (having just passed the little inlet for spring water) I turned to Glen and asked him why we didn't always receive the answers we were seeking. Rather quickly he replied, "I think it's because of fear. Fear gets in the way. We just need to deal with fear." That seemed like a logical answer and so our spiritual education continued.

Perhaps it was the quiet of the night that was so helpful (though daytime on the mountain was far from noisy). There's a mental stillness to be found when others are asleep. Whatever the reason, we certainly heard (though not with our physical senses) the angel messages intended for us. Instead of the physical sense of seeing, hearing, taste, touch and smell, spiritual sense includes such qualities as hope, faith and understanding.

Staying with the spiritual side of existence is like playing in the right ball park. So, let's go to four different games in which spiritual sense comes up to bat as a witness. Now these four games, like all baseball games, start at home base. The first game appropriately has to do with home—our mountain home. But first a few words about home runs.

Home runs.

If we expect to make a home run on our mental journey Spiritward, our progress can't be judged by whether the path is smooth or rough and whether the good things we deserve come to us or not. Sometimes the argument is made, "Well, it's only right to have things go smoothly isn't it!" Looking and waiting for that smooth result (heaven forbid we should have to slide into home base!) is human reasoning based on the material senses. It's the wrong question. The question of progress and the spiritual goal need to be uppermost so we can't be swayed by the scenery along the way (whether it's pleasant or rugged).

Peter gave Jesus that kind of argument, the one for the peaceful path, when Jesus told them of the coming crucifixion. With his typical impetuosity and from a human view of what was divinely good, Peter rebuked Jesus saying, ". . . Be it far from thee, Lord: this shall not be unto thee" (Matthew 16:22). Evidently Peter thought he knew the Father's business better than did Jesus. Bless his heart! And moreover, Peter's rebuke infers that if things work out well we are on the right track. It also implies, conversely, that if one doesn't encounter smooth sailing there is something wrong—either with our work or with the divine Principle on which we base our work. The topic is still timely. In fact, someone asked us a question along the same lines when we purchased the little home on the mountain.

In God we trust . . . or a deed of trust?

When Glen and I moved to the mountain it was at a time when real estate had taken a dip. We felt spiritually impelled to live on top of the mountain. It was our next classroom on our spiritual journey, of that we felt certain. So we went ahead with

156

our plans and took quite a loss on the property we sold. A well-meaning acquaintance asked me about the transaction and how we had profited. When I confessed the loss, she exclaimed, "What kind of a demonstration is that!" She apparently expected God's goodness to be demonstrated in monetary success, suggesting that taking a loss would signify failure. I replied, "We call it obedience."

When Glen first contacted the owner who appeared on the county records, the man said he didn't really own the property anymore, believing his ex-wife had given his share to his son-in-law. That didn't seem possible. On looking into the matter, he found out that he did indeed own half the property with his relative to whom he had not spoken for years. So a healing of that rift followed Glen's inquiries and the owners agreed to sell the property to Glen because they trusted him. They even accepted Glen's fair assessment of the worth of the property, but they would not accept Realtors as part of the sale process.

We had asked to be given a deed of partial reconveyance to the property so that we might sell off a small portion of this large acreage, but the owners (desiring to keep the transaction simple) were unwilling to do so. We decided it felt right to go ahead with the purchase anyway.

Interestingly, when sitting in the escrow office preparing to finalize the sale, it became apparent to us that there were actually two parcels of property being sold as one. Upon seeing the two tax statements, we then asked if we could divide the purchase price between the two properties and this was amenable to the owners who would carry the paper on it. So we purchased the two properties, each with their own deed of trust. Then we immediately sold off the first little acre and cabin at the roadside to a mountain friend of ours for the exact price as the loss on the other house. This was a nice "added" benefit but it was definitely not our goal, and certainly not something by which to judge the rightness of our actions.

If we had not been willing to take what looked like a loss on the property we sold, then we would never have gone to the mountain. Such a move wouldn't have looked humanly advantageous. That was Peter's problem when he found out about the impending crucifixion. His assessment of the situation facing Jesus was definitely along the lines of not taking a loss.

Jesus' stinging reply to him set the scene straight. "Get thee behind me Satan: thou art an offence unto me: for thou savorest not the things that be of God, but those that be of men" (Matthew 16:23, Mark 8:33). This incident is recounted in two of the four Gospels. The only other time Jesus used that phrase, "Get thee behind me Satan," was on the mountain when refusing the temptation to rule the kingdoms of the world by worshipping matter. He chose instead to worship Spirit.

Jesus' strong words rebuked human reasoning. Peter's human view denied that anything so bad should happen to a man so good. Jesus' spiritual view was that he was carrying out a divine mission, showing us the pathway out of a fleshly, limited, material sense of existence, not trying to get comfortable in it. This subject is so beautifully dealt with in the chapter "Atonement and Eucharist" in *Science and Health* that it is difficult to choose a single quotation. Here are two selections from pages 40 and 41. "Was it just for Jesus to suffer? No; but it was inevitable, for not otherwise could he show us the way and the power of Truth."

And, "The nature of Christianity is peaceful and blessed, but in order to enter into the kingdom, the anchor of hope must be cast beyond the veil of matter into the Shekinah into which Jesus has passed before us; and this advance beyond matter must come through the joys and triumphs of the righteous as well as through their sorrows and afflictions. Like our Master, we must depart from material sense into the spiritual sense of being."

(Shekinah in Westminster's Bible Dictionary signifies the presence of God.)

Publish the book!

It appeared that some "sorrows and afflictions" would accompany my path for awhile because it was only eight years after we left the mountain that Glen passed on. The loss seemed twofold in that a wonderful love was no longer visible and (perhaps even more importantly) my spiritual traveling companion, my classmate, was now making progress on the other side of humanity's horizon.

Ours was such an obviously close union that a friend had asked, somewhat facetiously, if we intended to leave this world together. I spoke with Glen about it. What if one of us were to leave and the one remaining couldn't follow right away? What would we do? He simply said, "We've always been as obedient as we know how. We would just go on being obedient."

This did not prove, in my case, to be as simple as it sounded. It seemed as though I were perched precariously on the edge of a pit, knowing I shouldn't go near it or fall in, yet not always able to retreat. I clung to the facts of Life, its eternality and goodness. And when needed, on occasion, I was helped by a loving friend to hold onto those facts.

The "never trapped" lesson was helpful too because there was a way to bear the situation, as Paul promised. My dear daughter and I became roommates for awhile until she married. Her love and care were part of God's love being shown me. She also become my computer tutor for an important project.

Soon after Glen left I prayed earnestly (actually almost desperately) for an answer. What should I do next? Three words came to me as strongly as if they had been spoken out loud, "Publish the book!"

A month or so prior to this I had felt impelled to write down a story, an allegory, which was suddenly flooding into my thinking. This was totally unplanned and I literally did not know each day what the next chapter would be. It came a chapter a day each morning. When I had completed nine chapters I realized this contained many of the spiritual lessons Glen and I had worked on, but there was one in particular that wasn't included. I prayed for this and, in another day or two, I was given the last chapter.

During this time, Glen told me that he had a dream one night that something important was taking place and that it should be supported. He then held up the manuscript and commented, "I think this may be it!"

However, when the command to publish the book was given, I knew it referred to my dad's manuscript that lay unfinished when he had passed on fifteen years before. He had been urged to write this by my stepmother, a dear lady my dad married two years after my mother had passed on right as he commenced his lecture tours. This true, spiritual adventure story began with his capture and subsequent imprisonment for three years in Java during WWII, a period he would refer to as, "When I was a guest of the Japanese." He also related events after the war to do with employment and the United Nations.

Up to this time, I'd shrugged off people's queries about the book with comments such as, "Well, if it had been meant to be finished and published, surely that would have occurred." Smart human observation, but not necessarily true! Now, with such an answer to my prayer, I had no other choice than to rethink the human reasoning and be obedient to the divine command.

This involved setting up my own company—no small task and one for which I had no human training. It seemed as though three decades in the healing practice of Christian Science was not the quickest route to the publishing business and yet, of course, in a way it prepared me for everything I had to do next.

Only a few months after Glen's passing, my daughter and I moved into an apartment together, where she taught me the rudiments of the computer. Off to work she'd go while I made my way through a maze of headers and footers, page numbering and all else included in providing the printing company with a camera-ready copy of the manuscript.

Many are the tales I could tell and bore you completely, so I'll try to avoid the details. But you can imagine how it felt during just one such computer adventure when my printer didn't seem compatible with the fonts used in this early DOS program and started to print out what looked like Greek symbols on the very night before the manuscript was due to be sent off. My daughter even lovingly offered to go in and change all the fonts but I prevented her and prayed a little harder. The next morning I was given two totally clean manuscripts, in English, by the now-cooperating printer.

The book arrived the week of the D-Day anniversary in 1994 and hit the mental beachheads as, *The Ultimate Freedom*. It came out just nine months after Glen's departure. And the rest, as they say, is history.

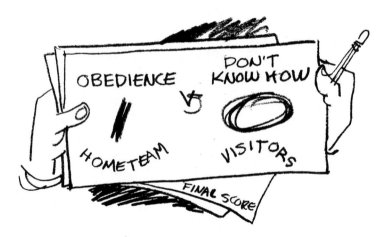

The material senses testified to fading good and the loss of a wonderful relationship . . . but spiritual sense told me otherwise—about my relationship to God, which could never be interrupted. In obedience to this heavenly Parent, uninterrupted goodness won the day!

The language of Love.

The book sold out of its first printing of five thousand copies in only seven months. Though the pace has slowed since then, the book continues steadily along virtually by word of mouth. It is now out in four languages and on cassette too. Each experience with the book has been a wonderful adventure in itself, though at times a trifle challenging due to various circumstances. I'd like to relate just one instance from each translation to show how beautifully the quiet answers came—and always on time!

The first instance had to do with the Spanish translation by an excellent editor, with strong language and writing skills of her own. A native of Argentina, she undertook the first translation of the book with joy and diligence. We agreed on most points, though I must have tried her patience by questioning various aspects as we went along, such as the conversion of passive tense into active. My translator patiently faxed me sections from grammar books and the reasons involved. However, when it came to "palo grande" I dug in my heels. (I'd better explain that I was reading the Spanish from a background of four years of high school Latin. Though it worked for me it must have made the translator's job a little more difficult!)

Now, the "palo grande" incident took place in the prison camp, when a guard had approached my dad in a threatening manner with a two-by-four. This is a good-sized piece of wood but there was no Spanish equivalent for it and the translator wanted to use simply "palo grande"—big stick. But would this ring true from a man's perspective? We were now approaching metaphysical territory that Glen and I had explored extensively.

Since the 1960s and the unisex trend, it was not uncommon to hear or read of a blend of male and female in one person. The

163

blend became very obvious to us and we even mentioned it to an editor of a religious publication, saying we felt it imperative to keep the divine distinction intact. She smiled patiently and remarked we were talking like two people who had just been married (which in fact we had). But that wasn't the point at all. We were really talking as two metaphysicians regarding the distinction of true manhood and true womanhood that Christian Science makes in support of the spiritual account of creation found in the first chapter of "Genesis."

Though male and female might possess qualities in common—such as wisdom, purity, love and strength—their mental genders each maintained a distinct character. The blurring or blending of their individual characters on the divine scene could only wreak havoc on the human scene if one were to employ that blend as a life principle by which to live.

That's why I didn't like "palo grande"—big stick. I felt it would not be correct from a man's point of view. Perhaps this was too fine a point but because it seemed so important to honor the distinctness of all of God's creation, I asked the translator to talk it over with her husband, also a native-Spanish speaker. The final "poste de madera" (wooden post) was acceptable to all of us. And so *La libertad absoluta* was ready to set sail!

There's an interesting postscript to this story. A few years later, this same editor asked me to write an article on the subject of male and female for the Spanish magazine she edited. And because she also formatted the Russian and German translations of *The Ultimate Freedom,* she was able to format a very important Russian book for her publishing company. The ripples were going out in more ways than one.

The Russian translation came next. The translator has since said to me, when throwing out the large stack of fax correspondence that had traveled between us, "It would be of no interest to anyone but us." Yes, there was much background work to the book, but the translator had an amazing background or life story of her own. Brought from Russia into the United States as a baby, she grew up and was schooled here. While revisiting Russia with her two small children, the Iron Curtain came down. This woman became trapped for thirty years in that country before returning again to the United States. Totally bilingual with strong writing and translating experience, and with a meticulousness that far surpassed even my own close attention to detail, the Russian translator was indeed a "find." As the Spanish translator said, with a smile in her voice, "She's even pickier than you are!" And how grateful I was for that—it being impossible for me to check on the Russian language.

When this translation was almost ready for the printer, the translator's daughter had just that week arrived in Boston from Russia to visit her mother. On seeing the Russian title of the book, she remarked that the Russian word used for "ultimate" had become, over the last year, adopted by the underworld. It now had a criminal connotation! We were literally saved at the last minute. The problem word was then replaced with one meaning "true" which could not be corrupted and, with its new title, the Russian translation went to press.

Generous individuals donated half the cost of the first edition of one thousand copies. With the dedication, "To Russia with love," these books traveled the ocean as a gift to the Russian people. (No, the James Bond movie was *From Russia with love*.) As well as being shared with people in four different locations,

165

including the Ukraine, the book has been gratefully accepted into the library system of the Universal Academy of Science, Art and Culture in St. Petersburg, and is available in fourteen of their branches for their many readers.

And then came the "German baby," as I called it. This took over twice the time required for the other translations as it appeared there were a few minefields in the way. My translator, a German native and writer of witty newspaper columns (in addition to being an excellent translator), has lived for decades on the East Coast of the United States. We felt it would be wise to have additional help in Germany, and so a young woman, an English teacher, with no working knowledge of Christian Science was found. With her uninitiated youthful approach, she was a perfect counterbalance to the translator's longtime immersion in the subject. Rather importantly, she was also up-to-date on the current German language. "Current" was one of the minefields as the German language had recently undergone a revision in which some spelling and punctuation rules had been simplified.

Another question involved a newer translation of *Science and Health*, which had met with a mixed response. Some did feel that certain words or phrases had been improved by the newer translation but maintained that other words carried a truer meaning in the old. As *The Ultimate Freedom* contains quotations from *Science and Health* you can see we had our work cut out for us. There were basically three challenges—not necessarily in order of importance but in order of appearance. First, the linguistic duty to honor the German-speaking populace in the use of their own language. Secondly, the need to support as best as possible the newer translation of *Science and Health*. Thirdly, to stay true to the meaning of Mrs. Eddy's discovery, which was vital.

With some larger questions settled, we then arrived at a special quotation from *Science and Health* (p. 494): "Divine Love always has met and always will meet every human need." I struggled over this because the word "need" was originally translated "Not"—a close approximation, whereas in the newer translation the German word appeared as "Bedarf," which to many carried a more commercial sense of "demand," as in supply and demand. How could we quote from the new translation and still retain the better meaning?

I prayerfully asked that question. The quiet answer appeared with the clue being found in my dad's book where he speaks of this quotation appearing on the walls of churches. I suddenly realized that statement would appear on the walls of the German churches in the older form, with "Not" for need. I could use the older version with accuracy—both physical accuracy (what was on the walls) and metaphysical accuracy (the meaning to be conveyed). How grateful I was for this quiet answer.

The foregoing is not intended as any type of criticism but simply to show what was involved and how divine Love does cover all the bases for a home run! With help from a native-German-speaking friend, we proofed the German together. God always gives us what we need and, though I had no education in German, some knowledge of Dutch was enough to help me in the proofing. And so *Die wahre Freiheit* went to press. Yes, the true help was always the divine Mind, which showed clearly what was needed at the time. And I'm grateful the translators were more than patient with my exploration into their native languages. My dear German translator said I almost drove him to distraction on a number of occasions. Then he kindly and gallantly added, "But there was always a bedrock of reason!"

In working on the translations, I gained tremendous new appreciation for Mary Baker Eddy's accomplishment as she had to convey infinite, spiritual meanings while working with a finite, material system. She was actually translating divine concepts into human language. What a task! No wonder Mrs. Eddy spoke of having to impart spiritual truths "through the meagre channel afforded by language" (*Science and Health*, p. 460).

The Ultimate Freedom in its various languages has helped introduce and re-introduce the wonderful living truths found in the Bible—truths which are spiritually, scientifically explained in *Science and Health*. Because the author of *The Ultimate Freedom* has no personal or hidden agenda, the book is acceptable to those of any religion.

When this book was going out by the tubful, the containers were picked up by a young woman from the post office. She asked what I was mailing so I gave her a copy. One day she came to the door with tears in her eyes and an admission to make. She explained that she was a Christian who had held a prejudice against Christian Science. "But," she exclaimed, "it is so biblically oriented." When I met her on the street a year later, this young woman told me she was loaning *The Ultimate Freedom* to anyone who needed it!

So many are the stories of gratitude that have poured in from around the world as well as the heartwarming accounts from people in my local area to whom I've given the book. A woman took it to her Lutheran church and the choir all read the book, signing their names in the back of it. And a Spanish-speaking Catholic woman shared it with her large family and recounted how it had helped each one of them—solving a legal dispute, a custody battle and completely changing two people's characters.

Crossing all geographical and religious borders, *The Ultimate Freedom* has been welcomed into homes from Alaska to Australia and from the Seychelles (islands off the coast of Africa) to the Hawaiian Islands. It has warmed the hearts of those in Veterans' Administration hospitals and given hope to, and mentally liberated, many in prison. And it helped free me too—from the prison of grief. It is plain that the quiet answer, "Publish the book," was not specially for me. I feel it is one of the many answers that divine Love gives to the quiet questions that are asked about life, and this answer simply and lovingly included me as well.

As you can see, this third game won by spiritual sense sent ripples around the world proving there is a brotherhood already in place prepared to receive good ideas and pass them along. This brotherhood is formed and maintained by the heavenly Parent we have in common.

As an added note to the victory over grief, a few years ago I wrote this poem which may help another in a similar situation. I hope the illustrations may even bring a smile!

"Goodbye to Grief"

Today I said goodbye to grief
And, oh, this is a blessed relief,
For it really was no friend of mine
Though dropping by from time to time.

If I could keep busy, is what I thought,
Then the battle would be easily fought.
But when I had to pause awhile
There it was with sad, sweet smile.

So next I tried to run quite fast,
But what was it that just ran past?

It was grief by which
I was overtaken;
Through tears I saw
it was not forsaken.

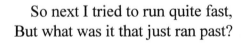

So, remaining still I stood my ground
And heavenly strength is what I found.
My Father-Mother always here,
Bid me come and face my fear.

And as I looked it in the face
I saw only Love, with its embrace.

The cloud had parted, then melted away.
I said goodbye to grief today.

Eine kleine Nachtmusik.

Perhaps we are still in a German mode or else Mozart's "A Little Night Music" best fits as a title for this section. After all, it *was* a little music and it *was* at night, but I'll need to fill you in on a number of details first. The other book I was writing, just before Glen passed, was published. *Numberland* came out in 1995, as did the true story *Bird*, which took place on Palomar Mountain. The publishing of my dad's book in fact opened the way for the other two. But there's more to this story. A song had come to me at the same time *Numberland* was flooding into my thinking. Having had two or so years of piano lessons when I was about twelve years old, I dimly recalled where certain notes went on the staff but I knew nothing of writing timing or value for these notes. As the music continued to come I realized that *Numberland* was also going to be a musical.

My short piano playing career, though perhaps quite adequate, had not been particularly brilliant and composing music was not even a dim consideration, let alone a desire of mine. My piano teacher had at one time said to my mother, "Auriel would keep playing if the roof fell in." I believe that was the closest thing to a compliment that I heard and of course it had more to do with tenacity than with the piano. So, you can imagine how startled I was to have this music suddenly floating around. I would pick out the notes on my daughter's keyboard and put the "blobs" (as I called them) on the musical staff. Then somehow my left hand would find chords and I'd look them up to see what I was playing.

After recording the piece on my boom box, I would take it to the arranger who, like the artist with the fax machine, brought out a beautifully arranged piece of work. I would usually sit there the whole time and give input during the arranging process. At one point I noticed a few notes were wrong on the sheet music and mentioned this fact, but the arranger assured me that was exactly what I was playing and singing on the tape. I replied, "Oh my goodness, you can't listen to my playing and singing, you've got to look at the blobs on the paper!" Is this enough to give you an idea of what went on in the music production department? This was definitely not so much a composing as a listening adventure.

The adventure continued as I found a recording studio manned by "J. the Genius" (as I call him). My daughter introduced me to two friends, husband and wife, who were in musical theater and who had wonderful singing voices. In fact, rumor had it that the husband did "a better Robert Goulet than Robert Goulet." These friends in turn brought in other singers and that's how some local musical theater leads sang bit parts on the first *Numberland* CD. Producing this CD was another large learning experience as you can imagine.

After the first *Numberland* CD of music and dialogue was published, friends said that one song in particular should have a longer version. This could be done, I reasoned, if I just had a bridge for the song, but nothing came to me. One night, after I'd gone to sleep, I heard a knock at my door. No one was there. It happened again and again. Still no one was there. "What am I doing standing around here at midnight?" was the question I asked myself and immediately heard an answer. "Go to the keyboard!" As I let my fingers run over the keys, the needed bridge for the song came and so I put my usual blobs on the musical staff and went back to bed.

The next session with the arranger was a long one of about five hours, and towards the end I mentioned that I had a new and longer version for one song but didn't know what I'd do with it.

I didn't even care much for the new lyrics I'd written. As the arranger scanned the lyrics I could see he wasn't much interested in them either, but he worked on the bridge, building the song to a new level. I remember sitting on the floor and listening while he made this layer-cake of music, adding various instruments until it reached its final peak. As this music became multi-dimensional and swirled around the room through the two large speakers, I took paper and pencil and wrote new lyrics, while still sitting on the floor. A couple of verses were added later to complete "It's forever that I love you," heaven's love song to us.

This entailed rewriting some of the musical and adding the song, now sung by the teacher to the pupils to describe how the perfect principle of numbers loves every number. This song has since been sung at church services and at weddings and I continue to hear reports of how it has touched others and even healed broken hearts. How could all of this have been possible? It still amazes me. I feel as though I simply opened a window and the music flew in. I've never had the sense of composing it.

If someone had told me in 1993 that the very next year I would be in the publishing business and that from 1996 on I would be doing such things as: standing on a street corner taping traffic noises; recording a police siren—kindly turned on for me by a police woman; taping bird songs in a pet store . . . and all for CDs for which I had written music and lyrics, well, I would have been more than astounded. Indeed, I would have thought the individual telling me this fantastic story was in dire need of professional help. But all those activities, and many more, actually took place.

Perhaps you'll agree this proves it is impossible to plan the events of our lives. I know it's popular to encourage people to visualize what they want and sometimes that very thing seems to occur. But that's just the human scene yielding to the human desire. It's like actors changing a script instead of going to the author for needed input. The Principle of our life doesn't even appear on that playbill. How much more satisfying to listen to divine Love's purpose for each one of us. And how necessary that obedience is if we are going to progress on our spiritual journey.

We need heavenly direction to arrive at the spiritual consciousness called heaven. We may even be asked to do things we've never done before, but that simply turns what might, at times, seem like an arduous journey into a spiritual adventure. I certainly found that out in so many ways.

The full impact of producing the CDs finally hit home after a couple of things happened at the studio. On one occasion, a group of men came in as I was leaving and they laughingly called out to the engineer, "Hey, give her the job." I wanted to tell them I *was* the job. Then another time as I was sitting beside J. at the console working, a friend of his came in and casually began to chat with him. After a minute or two he looked over at me and asked J., "Is this your mother?" As we continued to stare at him, he changed his question to, "Your girlfriend?" At that point, I told him I was the producer.

Thinking this over, I finally asked my engineer, "How many women sit in this chair, producing?" He replied, "Oh, about one in twenty." So, only five percent were women producers. I was being asked to do something which was not only unusual for me to do but which was also unusual for most women. I'm glad I didn't know that in advance! But it does prove that God is certainly an equal-opportunity employer.

During the taping of the first CD, I remember driving home at midnight, in tears, saying to myself, "I have no one to talk to about this" and hearing the reply, "You can talk to me." It was true. I could and did talk it over with God and the answers always came. In one instance, I had to include the dialogue and music about minus signs before the project could continue smoothly. Another time, when one line of dialogue was lost in a multitude of dialogue, it was like the proverbial needle in a haystack. The quiet answer came quite quickly and the sentence was found.

So many are the stories that could be told about the musical side of my spiritual pathway, but I won't burden you with details except for one more night-music episode. It all began in the daytime when I was given complimentary theater tickets by two dear friends. While standing in the office to redeem my tickets, a young man came in on some theatrical business and began to talk with me. He asked what I did and when I mentioned that I was about to cut a new CD, this young man told me he was a singer and offered to give me his name and phone number. He further mentioned that his wife also sang and that on occasion he worked with a group of children at a song and dance studio in Orange County.

With complete confidence that my project was all set, I told my new acquaintance that I didn't really have a need but I took the information anyway—more out of politeness than anything else.

Two weeks later, on the first night of taping the new CD, "Something Bright and Beautiful," the baritone selected for two songs could hit the high notes in one song but not in the other. So, I found the piece of paper and asked the young man to audition, with my arranger being present. As he sang, his beautiful voice floated through my screen door all over the neighborhood. The arranger and I looked at each other startled. Then the singer suggested we hear a CD of a recent show. We found ourselves listening to the National Touring Company of *Beauty and the Beast* and he was playing the Beast! His wife had played Beauty for awhile on Broadway and on tour for three years with him. Oh, yes. He'd do just fine!

This was a beautiful illustration of Jesus' statement, ". . . your Father knows what things ye have need of, before ye ask him" (Matthew 6:8), and also the biblical promise found in Isaiah (65:24), "And it shall come to pass, that before they call, I will answer; . . . ." I was given this answer before I even knew there was a need. (Try to visualize that!) But, what I've told you so far was only the beginning. So much more was yet to come!

Soon I found out there was a need for a new female lead singer and that's how the young woman who had played Beauty came to sing the title song, "Something Bright and Beautiful." And she more than lived up to that title!

All was going well for this CD until I learned that the scheduled group of children would not be available to sing at an upcoming session. Remarkably, I was extremely calm when hearing this news, feeling that an excellent answer was at hand. I remembered that my new singer, who played the Beast, had worked with a children's group in Orange County but I couldn't reach him. However, the exact company name floated into mind and, after calling Directory Assistance, I left a message asking if they could provide me with children to tape two songs only eight days away.

Very shortly, I received a call back, saying they could provide me with the children and that I should bring the music over immediately. Good idea! But where was I going? You see, I live just outside the northern tip of Orange County and J's studio is only six miles south of me, just inside the County which stretches for miles below his location. Yes, Orange County covers a large area—948 square miles, which is two-thirds the size of the state of Rhode Island—so obviously I was wondering just where this song and dance studio might be located. Before I could ask, they asked me where I taped my sessions and I gave them the street name and the number, 5811. There was a pause and the school's director said, "We are at 5860." Yes, they were almost directly opposite the studio and the children could simply walk across the street for the recording sessions!

But this was not two human situations that happened by chance to coincide. The coincidence that makes a real difference is when human desires, plans or hopes yield to the divine plan. To the extent that the human coincides (agrees) with the divine, to that extent does God's loving care become visible on the human scene. This coincidence isn't mysterious or unexplainable but spiritually scientific and provable. Yes, in even the smallest details of our lives. Again, using mathematics, it is like an individual agreeing with the invisible math facts and seeing the harmony this coinciding produces. The harmony in this case was one of music, so let's take up the story again.

I took the music to the song and dance studio and was asked to return later that evening. This was my second special encounter with some "night music" and it might have been a scene from a movie. Light spilled out of the open studio door onto the dark parking lot and, as I approached, the sweetest little voices could be heard singing one of my songs. These children subsequently sang songs for the new musical *Musicland* and are featured on a number of my CDs. That wonderful night introduction to the children remains a high point for me. With lovely characters, they are definitely a sign of a turning tide.

May I tell you just one of the instances which so impressed me? When taping those first two songs, the session went on for four hours, during which the children became a little tired. Their parents, who had been patiently waiting in the tiny reception room, sprang into action and left to buy fruit and other refreshing goodies for them.

Then children took turns trying out for one solo line of singing in the glass isolation booth at the back, while the others stood in line in the main studio. Their director told them not to look back at the child singing, but as soon as each child finished the others immediately turned round and applauded. So many wanted to try out, but time was short and I told the children we had to finish. With not one grumble but with smiling faces, they picked up their belongings and went past me in single file with a resounding "**thank you**." Experiences like this help to convince one that the greatest talent is that of a beautiful character.

Though humanly surprising, I don't consider any of these experiences to be miraculous. They were divinely natural ways of providing what was needed and even before the need was apparent. It was when preparing for the taping of "Lessons from Bird" that I went through an open house and met a Realtor who just happened to know, by heart, the telephone number of a man involved in a community musical theater group. I called and he came over to visit. He, in turn, gave me the demo tape of a woman with an amazing voice (she had played Grisabella in *Cats* on Broadway for almost four years). This talented singer and I subsequently became friends and she agreed to sing "The Language of Love" on my upcoming CD. When in the studio for the taping, I remarked to her encouragingly, "Think of that wonderful demo!" She immediately replied, "I'm thinking of the Holy Spirit."

So, whether Broadway stars, local musical theater stars, or children with the gift of talent and character, all that was needed was there on time and, very importantly, everyone had the right spirit for the work!

When speaking of receiving necessary supply, my dad made the statement in *The Ultimate Freedom* (p. 111) that although supply may come *through* people it does not come *from* people. All that is truly good is always from God, who has infinite resources for all His creation. I believe it was that conviction —that the music and the ideas in these projects were from God not from me—which opened the door to receiving the talented singers, musicians/arrangers, and sound engineer that were needed.

You may notice that spiritual sense just won all four games it played while the material senses struck out in their one and only game allowed. But this is not an equal-opportunity book for the limited side of life. One game in the wrong ballpark should be enough to move us elsewhere.

Speaking of moving, I did consider that when visiting friends in another state after Glen passed on. But when the husband, who was in real estate, offered to show me some homes, all I could say to him was that I wanted to run home to Glen.

After reading these experiences, you might agree that I did make a home run to Glen in the best possible way. I'd turned homeward to God, to Life eternal, for it's in that Life we all dwell together.

In each of these instances, it was spiritual sense that saved the day. The material senses testified to loss and unhappiness all the while the spiritual senses were testifying to everpresent good (which can never be lost), to inspiration and answers that are at our mental fingertips, and to wonderful new spiritual adventures that are just around the corner. And now, I'd like to leave this subject on a very grateful and homeward note.

A Light in the Window

"Thy word is a lamp unto my feet,
And a light unto my path." *
Yes, there's a light in the window I see
There's a light that's been left on for me.

When the world I did roam,
Knew not where to call home,
There was a light in the window for me.

Though the years flitted by
In the wink of an eye,
Still unflickering that light was for me.

And when night seemed so sad
It was hard to be glad,
Shone on the light in the window for me.

Yet, when day sparkled bright
There was one brighter light,
It was that light in the window I see.

Now the window is much nearer
And the path so much clearer,
Because of the light in the window, you see.

I thank you God, my Father-Mother,
No matter how scenes changed
And my life was rearranged,
You left that light on, in the window, for me.

*Psalm 119:105

Christly counsel.

Our world, and certainly the society in which we live, seems firmly attached to evidence obtained from our senses, from the seeing of the eye and the hearing of the ear. There exists, however, a large number of relatively fearless and humble people who deal quite easily with the material, physical senses—people who don't necessarily believe what they see and will expect the seemingly impossible to be possible.

This group is not congregated in any one region or country but is spread throughout the world. Not confined to any one religion, race or language, and with living conditions that could vary from extremely rich to extremely poor, this special sector of society possesses the natural ability to discount the physical senses.

By this time, you may already have guessed the direction we're taking here. Yes, we're talking about little children.

Christ Jesus loved little children and told us to emulate them. When asked by his disciples who would be greatest in the kingdom of heaven, Jesus basically told them their question was irrelevant because they weren't even going to get there with thinking like that. How could they arrive at the heavenly state of consciousness which knows only good—which is conscious of what God knows—with all the adult baggage they were dragging along. Unless they let go of human pride of position, reliance on matter instead of Spirit, their trust in the material senses to tell them what is spiritually good, they were not going to arrive at their spiritual goal.

It all came down to one word: humility. Humility makes way for and bows before the divine laws. It accepts no limitation on God's children, not because of human expertise or knowledge, but because of divinity's omnipotence, omnipresence and omniscience. Humility no more attributes special power to the image and likeness of God than it does to an image in a mirror, but acknowledges the source of all being and doing. Humility is kind and impartial. Humility listens and waits. It doesn't maintain a stockpile of evidence based on the material senses.

Little children naturally have humility because they have not been totally taken over by the physical senses, not yet convinced by the material world's degrading laws of limitation, nor deluded by false promises of grandeur. Children are usually quick to be healed because they readily receive good ideas. They also believe what adults say, so it is wise to be careful just what we tell them. Even a casual remark may be accepted as a possibility and this could account for what happened to a little boy named Jonathan.

The Queen comes to town.

When Jonathan was only about five, he was quite interested in the British Royal family. He lived in Southern California with his mother and that's quite a distance from Buckingham Palace so, of course, all that he saw of the Queen was either pictures in books or images on television.

One day Jonathan's mother, who is an educator, had to attend a special adult class. Finding no babysitter for Jonathan, she had no alternative but to take him with her. She told him how important this was to her and that he must be very good and quiet. So Jonathan took his stickers and coloring equipment and for the two hours he was, as the saying puts it, as good as gold. The other adults in the class even remarked on it. As they left, his mother praised his conduct and added, "Why, Jonathan, you were good enough to meet the Queen!"

Now it just so happened that, not long after, the Queen was scheduled to pay a visit to California, even to the general area in which Jonathan lived. A seventh-grade teacher, a friend of the family, planned to take some of her students to a location where they could see the Queen and invited Jonathan to go along. In fact, the teacher's daughter had been chosen to present a bouquet of flowers to the Queen.

Jonathan was totally delighted. He shined his shoes and dressed for the occasion in his best little Sunday-School suit. He was going to see the Queen. However, there was more than a glimpse in store for Jonathan. When it came time to hand the bouquet to the Queen, the little girl became very shy and a substitute presenter needed to be found. Of course, the logical choice was Jonathan, who was prepared and ready. And that's how Jonathan did indeed meet the Queen of England!

Photograph used by permission of the Kirshner family

I love this story because of the elements in it. The child's obedience opened doors for him. Jonathan went prepared for the occasion and with great respect. He had the courage to step up and do what was asked of him. And he must have accepted what could have appeared to him as a distinct possibility or even a parental promise, "You were good enough to meet the Queen!"

Oh, to be as a little child and have the humility to believe the heavenly Parental promises made to us: "For I the Lord thy God will hold thy right hand, saying unto thee, Fear not: I will help thee" (Isaiah 41:13). "For ye shall go out with joy, and be led forth with peace . . . " (Isaiah 55:12).

Where to look for answers.

Where does a humble, trustful child look for answers? Usually to a parent whom it plies with questions. Unashamed of not knowing and with a thirst to understand the world around it, a little child meets with high adventure every day. "Why is the sky blue?" "What makes the snow?" Or sometimes it's a more technical question, as my four-year old son asked while viewing a live band performance in a park. He stared for some time at the band shell, which appeared small in the distance, then turned to me with great wonder and the telling question, "Where do they plug it in and how do they turn it on?" People within earshot all had a good laugh and undoubtedly guessed that the child's entertainment had been mostly from television.

One thing is certainly true. Children do not look within themselves for an answer. The rather popular concept to "look within yourself" can be misleading. If it means that we can expect answers to come to human consciousness and that we'll recognize them as we meet them there, all well and good. But if it implies that the divine resides within the human, then we have problems.

A child, playing with various sizes of boxes, early on learns that it's impossible to put a larger box into a smaller one. Yet sometimes we, as adults, try to do that very thing. *Science and Health* (p. 467), using Spirit and Soul as synonyms for God, clearly explains this impossibility: "Science reveals Spirit, Soul, as not in the body, and God as not in man but as reflected by man. The greater cannot be in the lesser. The belief that the greater can be in the lesser is an error that works ill."

However, the human is not without divine help. Though the divine cannot be contained within the human, there does exist what Mary Baker Eddy referred to as "a divine influence ever present in human consciousness." It's this influence that, when we become quiet and listen, enables us to recognize the answer when it comes. This influence is our receiving apparatus.

To ask our heavenly Parent for answers to our questions is the true and childlike solution. The Principle of life, which is God, good, has within its own Mind all that creation needs. Spirit has spiritual answers for its beloved sons and daughters. As humanity turns to this Mind, we find better views of our true identity and of our heavenly Parent. Those who have exhausted every human means for happiness or health usually find they cannot make it on their own without divine guidance and input. As *Science and Health* explains (p. 332): "Christ is the true idea voicing good, the divine message from God to men speaking to the human consciousness." Though the answers may come *to* human consciousness, they do not come *from* human consciousness.

Our rather regular disappointments are like "home movies" produced by our own misconceptions of Life—movies where happiness and success keep fading in and out as though the camera is out of focus. No wonder *Science and Health* (p. 264) points us in another direction: "The crude creations of mortal thought must finally give place to the glorious forms which we sometimes behold in the camera of divine Mind, when the mental picture is spiritual and eternal. Mortals must look beyond fading, finite forms, if they would gain the true sense of things. Where shall the gaze rest but in the unsearchable realm of Mind?" (p. 264)

"Unsearchable" is an interesting choice of words. But it has to be true that, just as pride cannot enter the kingdom of heaven, the material senses can neither search for, nor in, the realm of the divine Mind. We can't peer into the metaphysical or non-physical by physical means.

Chasing the spiritual through the material will never be successful. What an impact Jesus' statement must have had in his day and still would to those looking for a physical or geographical location: "Neither shall they say, Lo here! or, lo there! for the kingdom of God is within you" (Luke 17:21). *Science and Health* (p. 576) supports and explains the metaphysical location that Jesus indicates: "This kingdom of God 'is within you,'—is within reach of man's consciousness here, and the spiritual idea reveals it."

A little word can make a BIG difference.

The little word "in" is one of the sticking points or challenges to Christian metaphysics today. All goodness, talents, faculties, and abilities reside in the original, in God. As does an image in a mirror, the spiritual image and likeness of God reflects but does not contain these abilities. So, they could certainly not be contained within the human approximation of that spiritual likeness, as good as it may be. To sail with the tide of putting the greater into the lesser, the divine into the human, involves losing the idea of reflection—of man as the image and likeness of God. It also involves loss of the quiet answer we need to hear from our heavenly source. By maintaining the distinction of the greater and the lesser, we maintain the means of receiving answers and we can logically reason this through.

Spiritual man, being an idea of God, dwells in the divine Mind but is not absorbed by it. He always maintains his individuality and identity. If man became absorbed into God instead of reflecting God, there would be an "all-cause" universe without an effect. There would be no receiving end for the answers and no angel messages would be needed. (And if man brilliantly created himself or his own universe, why would he need any answers at all?)

On the other hand, if God were in man then cause would become lost in effect and the end result would be an "all-effect" universe with no cause. The quiet answers would have no source and so would not exist. But they do exist because even the mortal misconception of the divine creation, called the human condition, is lovingly embraced by the divine presence and power. God is not in man and He is certainly not in matter or in material, earthly elements.

Elijah the prophet, fleeing from the wrath of wicked Queen Jezebel, took refuge in a cave. A great wind passed by breaking even rocks into pieces, but "God was not in the wind." Then an earthquake shook the ground, but "God was not in the earthquake." After the earthquake a fire raged, but "God was not in the fire." And after the fire "a still, small voice" (I Kings 19:10-12).

No matter what elements rage around us—be they winds of human will, the earthquakes of fear, or the fires of hatred, bitterness or remorse—one can listen for the still, small voice that is outside of these human conditions. God is present and His quiet answers are always within reach of our consciousness.

Gazing into the divine Mind we find beautiful attributes of thought that demand our attention. When Peter and John (Acts 3:2-8) told the lame man to "look on us," the man complied, expecting them to donate something to his lameness. Instead Peter, extending his hand, lifted the invalid to his feet. The man, lame from birth, was instantly healed. No wonder he leaped as he walked, praising God. Every day, goodness, mercy and truth urge us to "look on us"—look on everything that is good, and receive the blessing, so that we too may jump for joy.

When Paul wrote the following to the Philippians, it was almost as though he had called a meeting to order and introduced a metaphysical motion into their midst—a motion that he expected to be accepted and acted upon:

> Finally brethren, whatsoever things are true, whatsoever things are honest, whatsoever things are just, whatsoever things are pure, whatsoever things are lovely, whatsoever things are of good report; if there be any virtue, and if there be any praise, think on these things (Philippians 4:8).

Science and Health (p. 261) virtually seconds the motion, adding the scientific result: "Hold thought steadfastly to the enduring, the good, and the true, and you will bring these into your experience proportionably to their occupancy of your thoughts."

Will "Spiritual Sense" please take the stand!

Surely, humanity will finally cease asking God to look at everything from our perspective—from a human, limited viewpoint—and instead we will desire to see and know what God sees and knows—to look at creation from God's viewpoint. So, an exchange will be necessary! We'll need a new set of witnesses.

By refusing the testimony of the material senses and by appealing to the divine Mind—the Supreme Judge—a witness for our defense comes forward. Spiritual sense faces this Judge with confidence, for, "Shall not the Judge of all the earth do right?" (Genesis 18:25). And we can trust this new witness, because: "What is termed material sense can report only a mortal temporary sense of things, whereas spiritual sense can bear witness only to Truth" (*Science and Health*, p. 298). This witness is sworn to "tell the whole truth and nothing but the truth."

If we are ever going to see the man and woman of God's creating, if we are ever going to witness our true spiritual being as the image and likeness of God, or if we are ever to understand real perfection and the infinite, immortal wonders of creation, then it will have to be through spiritual sense. Spiritual sense—the sense of Spirit—is the generic term for the spiritual senses, just as material sense—a sense of matter—is the generic term for the material senses.

Science and Health (p. 209) defines spiritual sense: "Spiritual sense is the constant, conscious capacity to understand God," and gives the step-by-step method of employing this sense (p.298): "Spiritual sense, contradicting the material senses, involves intuition, hope, faith, understanding, fruition, reality."

Do those instructions seem too abstract for our everyday world? This hardly sounds like a flight manual or an airline pilot's check list. But let's pause for a moment to consider the fact that if it were not for those very qualities of thought, a pilot would not have a list to check, nor a plane to fly.

Sitting by a fire in prehistoric times, a caveman might have looked far into the heavens and pondered the seemingly impossible—that perhaps one day man would fly. But the concept was out of his reach, not because the laws of aerodynamics were not present but because civilization had not evolved to the point of understanding those laws, or of using the available resources that could make his dream a reality. Inventing the wheel and many in between steps had to be taken first.

However, this **intuition** surfaced throughout the centuries and finally become **hope**, despite doubting comments such as, "If God had intended man to fly He would have given him wings." The doubters did not win the day because hope was already making the transition into something stronger. A firm **faith** that flight was indeed in our future took hold to the point where people were willing to underwrite the expense of many attempts to put man in the air.

I remember as a child seeing some of the historical newsreel footage and how we laughed as all kinds of strange-looking contraptions collapsed. But a better **understanding** finally prevailed and those "contraptions" were refined over a period of time until **fruition** appeared. Man was in the air! The **reality** could no longer be denied. Man is not earthbound. He is free to fly and soar as far as his thinking will allow him and today that's quite a distance.

Recent photographs of the multi-colored and beautiful Cone Nebula taken by NASA's Hubble telescope have the appearance of science fiction instead of science fact. But as the saying goes, "You ain't seen nothin' yet!" Mary Baker Eddy, from her standpoint of spiritual perception, made a number of predictions in the 1800s; one had to do with space travel: "The astronomer will no longer look up to the stars,— he will look out from them upon the universe . . . " (*Science and Health*, p. 125).

The aeronautical advance that has taken place—from early attempts of the Wright brothers (as of 2003 that was only one hundred years ago) to the landing on the moon—was accomplished in a very short span of time. It was during my grandmother's lifetime! And we can expect to see wonderful, spiritual advances during and after this earthly classroom. That's why it's so important to have spiritual sense on the witness stand. So let's go through that list again, but from a more spiritual perspective.

INTUITION: Isaiah promised (30:21): "And thine ears shall hear a word behind thee, saying, This is the way, walk ye in it, when ye turn to the right hand, and when ye turn to the left." The angel messages or intuitions we need are always available. Yes, spiritual intuition will be given us as we travel on our journey. This is sometimes described as a "sixth sense" when in actual fact it is first in line of the spiritual senses. We have departed from material sense to follow new leadings, which take us closer to the understanding of God.

Example: When working for a department store, a young man was asked to switch over, for just one day, to a department he hadn't worked in before and drive a truckload of furniture to a certain destination. As he was driving up a hill in a sparsely populated area, he suddenly became aware that the gas gauge in the diesel truck was on empty. The area was unfamiliar to him and in those days diesel fill-up was not always available. The young man had visions of being stuck in a remote area with an empty gas tank and a van full of furniture. So he prayed, asking for God's guidance.

Instantly the thought came to him, "Lean forward, look down." He disregarded this idea as useless and prayed again more earnestly. Again, the same message came, "Lean forward, look down." So he obeyed and from this new angle noticed a switch that had previously been hidden from his view. At this point he had an inkling as to what it might be, so he flicked the switch over. The gas gauge immediately went back up to full! Yes, the truck had dual gas tanks—a fact no one had mentioned to him.

As you can imagine, a rather grateful young man accomplished his delivery and with a strong sense of God's everpresence. One thing this story so effectively proves: When listening for an angel message, there are no irrelevant angels! "For he shall give his angels charge over thee, to keep thee in all thy ways" (Psalm 91:11).

HOPE: "Blessed is the man that trusteth in the Lord, and whose hope the Lord is" (Jeremiah 17:7). Putting one's hope in God is the way of wisdom because hope in the human scene leads to continual disappointment, whereas hope in divinity takes us to the next important step, on to faith. Hope (as well as faith) is listed as a moral stage of development in *Science and Health* (p. 115), so we might come to the rather unusual conclusion that hopelessness is an immoral state. We tend to avoid those who express this sentiment or else we try to uplift them. It's obvious that fear has to be overcome and trusting in God's goodness is a great thought changer and fear remover: "As human thought changes from one stage to another of conscious pain and painlessness, sorrow and joy,—from fear to hope and from faith to understanding,— the visible manifestation will at last be man governed by Soul, not by material sense" (*Science and Health*, p. 125).

Example: After the Spanish translation of *The Ultimate Freedom* was finished, I made arrangements to travel down the coast to the home of an individual who would proofread the manuscript. She faxed me a wonderful diagram of directions, which I put into a plastic sleeve and filed in my "Directions" folder.

On the scheduled day, I loaded up the car and finally looked in the folder but the directions weren't there! Then followed what Glen would refer to as a "frantic search." Still nothing! Yes, I even prayed about it. No meaningful answer! So I gave in, called the woman at her office, confessing my mistake, and hastily scribbled down more directions. Not only had my hopes for an orderly exit vanished in the pressure to be on time, but my prayers seemed unanswered.

On returning to the garage, I suddenly remembered what Glen had said about fear obscuring an answer. Well, I was no longer fearful about getting lost so I did something that would appear quite unnecessary. I prayed again, "Dear Father-Mother, God, please show me where those directions are." Immediately, I mentally heard, "In the lawyer's file." So I went back inside and opened the file drawer. The lawyer had been employed only once for a copyright issue and that file had never been opened again—or so I thought. There were the directions, the very first sheet of paper in the file. The trip that day was memorable, more for the spiritual lesson learned than for the proofreading (the translation, of course, was excellent).

So this was a twofold lesson, proving that the answer is always present, and that it cannot be hidden when fear is released. Spiritual sense is truly the best witness!

FAITH: "Now faith is the substance of things hoped for, the evidence of things not seen" (Hebrews 11:1). Faith is actual substance—what a thought! Faith appears to be a pivotal point in spiritual sense because it is right at this point that the material senses are being denied and our evidence is being found elsewhere—in God who is Spirit. All the false evidence drummed up against humanity in order to convince us of sin, disease and death is being disputed at this stage of mental and spiritual development. It is as though a special gift is being unwrapped. *Science and Health* states (p. 297), "Faith is higher and more spiritual than belief. It is a chrysalis state of human thought, in which spiritual evidence, contradicting the testimony of material sense, begins to appear, and Truth, the ever-present, is becoming understood."

Example: With faith that their house would be sold that day, a woman had sent the rest of the family off to the beach. A larger home in their area had suddenly become available and the family had put down a deposit. Selling their own little home themselves would make the new purchase possible. To make the backyard more appealing to a prospective owner, her husband had begun to dig trenches for a needed sprinkler system.

As the sun was setting, the woman watched a car enter her cul-de-sac, pause in front of their "For Sale" sign and then drive slowly away. Now, as the last prospect of the day disappeared around the corner, the woman's hopes began to disappear too. Then suddenly the idea came to her to express joy. She was not going to place her faith on her hopes. Faith was higher in the scale of spiritual sense than hope. She had already expressed hope in God before taking that step of faith. Now, faith in God's goodness and provision was going to remain strong even when there was no physical evidence to support it. The woman remained at the window and began to rejoice that God always puts together His children for a right purpose.

A minute or two later that same car reappeared and the occupants came in to look at the house. After a day of fruitless house-hunting the group had felt just too tired to view one more home but, after going only a few blocks and for some unknown reason, they felt impelled to go back and look anyway. They bought the house that evening. When the woman's family returned, the buyer mentioned to the husband that he worked for a sprinkler company. There was no need to continue with trench digging as his company would put in the whole system for free.

UNDERSTANDING: When following the spiritual footsteps shown us by prophets, apostles and especially Christ Jesus, it becomes very apparent that we are continually being steered in the direction of understanding. Blind belief is "out." Steadfast faith is "in." Spiritual understanding is a "must."

"Understanding is a wellspring of life unto him that hath it" (Proverbs 16:22). On that firm basis, Jesus promised both freedom and eternal life. Impossible to want or have more than that! "And ye shall know the truth, and the truth shall make you free" (John 8:32). "This is life eternal, that they might know thee the only true God, and Jesus Christ, whom thou hast sent" (John 17:3). Jesus' words, and certainly his acts, imply that there is a divine Principle to be understood.

Understanding the truth of being is as different from faith as playing the piano by ear is different from understanding the theory or principle of music. There is nothing quite so comforting as this understanding. It brings security and the ability to put the principle consistently into practice.

Example: I had a healing of impacted wisdom teeth on the basis of faith and of understanding. Both lower teeth were under the gum and one was completely on its side according to x-rays. Dental surgery was suggested for their removal. The first lower impacted tooth appeared as I turned to God with great faith that He had always cared for my needs. The second tooth—the one on its side—did not appear until I gained the understanding that matter does not create, sustain or destroy harmony regarding our dental health. A good verdict as to dental or any kind of health cannot be based on material observation. Harmony is mandated by God, who is Spirit, in every facet of our lives and matter plays no part in determining harmony. As this recognition suddenly dawned on me, the second tooth emerged and in a totally upright position.

FRUITION: Jesus provides us with an infallible litmus test for all human thought and action: "Wherefore by their fruits ye shall know them" (Matthew 7:20). Hard to get around that one! Are we bringing forth the fruits of a false consciousness, of material sense, or the fruit of the Spirit? What effects do our thinking and actions have? What kind of a wake does our journey create behind us?

The fruitage or results of spiritual sense cannot be denied but they bear fruit of another dimension—that of Spirit. Paul explained it to the Galatians (5:22,23): " But the fruit of the Spirit is love, joy, peace, longsuffering, gentleness, goodness, faith, meekness, temperance: against such there is no law" (Galatians 5:22,23). No mortal theory of limitation, no human fear or false ideal can mandate against the fruit of the Spirit. Nor can we be robbed of the human manifestation of harmony that accompanies the fruit of the Spirit. The truth of being is always made practical in a way we can understand it.

Example: It was the faith and meekness involved in obeying the intuition to "lean forward, look down" that was the true fruit, and the full gas tank corroborated this fact. The meekness required by having to ask again for directions was the fruit of the Spirit—and the faxed directions became evident. Again, it was the faith, joy and peace of the woman that was her real fruitage—the home was simply the "added" or needed item which Jesus promised would appear as we seek first the kingdom of heaven. Likewise, faith, peace, and love of goodness were the fruits in the healing of the wisdom teeth, with the external evidence of right placement following closely behind.

Where does all this fruitage lead? It leads to our goal, the harmony termed the kingdom of heaven. It leads us to discover reality, the kingdom of God.

REALITY: The final question then has to be: Where will the kingdom of God be found in its all glory? It is exactly where Jesus told us it would be. It will be found in spiritual consciousness. This kingdom, unlike the kingdoms of the world, is full of heavenly peace and harmony. So, God's kingdom is not only the divine reigning supreme but it is also harmony reigning over all creation. This harmony will appear to us in degrees, in proportion to our spiritual growth. (Here again, metaphysics is not mysterious but quite understandable and practical.)

"Let unselfishness, goodness, mercy, justice, health, holiness, love—the kingdom of heaven—reign within us, and sin, disease, and death will diminish until they finally disappear" (*Science and Health* p. 248). If our consciousness is filled with goodness there is literally no room for the opposite of goodness to exist, so evil of any kind must diminish and disappear. A whole new view of creation is seen!

Example: St. John had a wonderful experience. "And I saw a new heaven and a new earth . . ." (Revelation 21:1). The fruit of the Spirit reveals a new heaven and earth—a whole new concept of life—which is entirely spiritual without beginning or end. How did John do this? Certainly not with his material senses. He had a better viewing medium.

A color-blind test in a college textbook helped me understand this. The page showed the word "onion" written in colored dots. However, those who couldn't see the red or green dots saw the word "color" written in different colored dots. Everyone was looking at the same page but some read a different word, according to their ability to see—or perceive—color.

Explaining John's revelation Mrs. Eddy wrote, "This testimony of Holy Writ sustains the fact in Science, that the heavens and earth to one human consciousness, that consciousness which God bestows, are spiritual, while to another, the unillumined human mind, the vision is material" (*Science and Health*, p. 573). John had the ability, through spiritual sense, to get a glimpse of reality. John was not spiritually color-blind.

How important spiritual sense is! May it take the witness stand for us each day of our journey, until we, like Dorothy in the *Wizard of Oz*, wake up to the fact that we never left home! Man is not an earthbound mortal but a spiritual being, free to roam the realm of Mind, God. But for now, let's continue with the journey.

What Do You Have in the House?

There's much more of value in one's house than you might expect. In this case, house means consciousness. On many occasions I've suggested to those looking for work that they make a list of their most employable qualities, such as accuracy, patience, honesty, punctuality, kindness and so on. And the work usually followed rather quickly. Therefore, the question as to what one has within the house is much more than merely making use of available materials at hand (which is always a good idea) but extends to the spiritual resources at our fingertips.

Two poor, richly-endowed widows.

The Biblical examples of how two widows received quiet answers are totally applicable to today's world. When the prophet Elijah asked a poor widow woman to prepare food for him, she replied she had only a handful of meal and a cruse of oil and was preparing to make something for herself and her son and then they would die.

But Elijah, who had already proved that God's goodness doesn't run dry, told her to take what she had at hand and use it to make him first a little cake and then feed her son and herself. The story goes on to relate that the meal never ran out nor did the cruse of oil fail. When the woman willingly, trustingly, unselfishly used what she had at hand it was more than enough.

The second story is about Elisha, who asked a poor widow (whose sons were about to be sold to pay a debt) what she had in the house? When she told him all she had was a pot of oil, Elisha said she should borrow many empty vessels and pour out oil and sell it to pay the debt. She obeyed and the pot of oil produced all that was needed. The woman had to bring in many vessels in order to make room for the abundance that was always on hand though it was not yet visible.

That's a wonderful lesson with a spiritual law behind it! God's goodness never fails, could no more be diminished than the sun could run out of sunbeams. What is needed is in fact always present. Our prayers do not make God more abundant than He already is, nor do they make our heavenly Parent more willing to love His children than He already is. With Him "there is no variableness, neither shadow of turning," as James told us.

So, we are not hoping for the divine Being to intervene in a human situation and rearrange it. That's baseless prayer. There is nothing behind it. That would be like praying for chalk to solve a problem on the blackboard without any principle of mathematics as a foundation for the answers. On the basis that there is a spiritual reality, we may ask that the truth of being—the harmony of God's universe—be made apparent. Then our prayers simply elevate us to a position, a spiritual vantage point, from which we can see the provision which already exists.

When his servant became concerned because the enemy forces coming up against them seemed so great, Elisha prayed and said, "Lord I pray thee, open his eyes, that he may see" (II Kings 6:17). Suddenly all the hills around them were full of chariots to protect them. The invisible good was made obvious to the young man. His spiritual sense took over.

Prayer is not simply having faith, but putting faith into action. We all have "something in the house." There is some work at hand, someone to help, a talent to be used. The willingness and gratitude involved in using what is at hand—our God-given talents, abilities or the work facing us—opens the door to more answers. In the chapter "Prayer," in *Science and Health*, is the statement, "If our petitions are sincere, we labor for what we ask; and our Father, who seeth in secret, will reward us openly " (p.13).

What a young woman with very little had in the house.

A young woman I knew years ago needed a job. Her husband (having just finished his military service) was likewise looking for work, and they had moved into a small, unattractive apartment. She was feeling rather discouraged but wanted to think spiritually about the situation. Perhaps I surprised her when I asked if there was any work on hand in the apartment. Had she unpacked? Had she arranged everything neatly in her closets? She admitted she hadn't and set to work tidying up.

After finishing, she noticed the bare window and thought if she could just buy a little remnant of fabric to put a valance across the top it would make the place more homey. With her apartment in order, she set off for a local fabric store where she had worked sometime previously. They were so happy to see her and asked if she would like to work there again. There was her job offer in a very short space of time. But she had already used what she had in the house, the work that was at hand, putting in order and beautifying her surroundings.

This is practical spirituality. The young woman put into action her love for God, good, even if it only meant a tidy closet. Man is always employed by God to reflect Him and God's universe is ever in order. So if we expect our bodies and our lives to be in good working order it would be only sensible to begin with what we can do right here, right now, in that direction. How can we humanly express or reflect the divine fact of order or employment? What resources do we have to bless another? Those are the actual questions we need to ask. And the answer is usually rather apparent.

What a teenager looking for work had in the house.

A similar situation took place with a teenager in my family. He was sixteen and trying a find an after-school job. And yes, he had even prayed about it. His mother suggested there was work to do around the house and yard jobs awaiting him.

She also reminded him that he needed to undertake that work, his contribution to the family, with good humor and willingness. Well this wasn't exactly the work he had in mind, and he wasn't sure how it would help him to find a job, but he did what she suggested and was able to accomplish his chores with a smile.

The very next day a friend of the family hired the teenager to do a little yard work and that same night when his mother returned home from a meeting she told him about a sign in a nearby ice-cream shop. It said, "Help wanted: female." The young man decided to apply anyway. They made an exception and gave him the job. So, within a day and a half of doing the work at hand, he had two jobs. In fact, he immediately found more part-time work at a paint store a few blocks from home, so that when the ice-cream shop closed down a couple of months

later he already had firmly established employment with all the hours he wanted at the paint store. And he so enjoyed this work!

Money matters?

Yes, we can take that title two ways, can't we! Matters could be a noun and simply signify that perhaps we are going to speak on the subject of money. Or else it might be a verb, which takes us in another direction to question whether money really makes a difference or not? Is money truly of consequence? It's difficult to judge another's point of view on that or any subject because: *(a)* one may be judging from one's own standpoint, or *(b)* appearances can be deceiving.

A friend lovingly informed me a few years ago that I had a hang-up with money and then recounted three different instances in which money had come up in our conversations. One instance had to do with giving someone their correct change, another with a copyright issue, and the last concerned a pricey seminar she was describing. Because of my comments, she had plucked money out of all three instances and figured that was the subject.

However, to me, the first had to do with accuracy, the second with lawfulness, the third with true value. There were three different subjects in my mind, and money was not the main topic in any one of them. What often appears to be a question of money—equal pay for equal work, for example—is actually about a much deeper issue. And to solve the question, the deeper issue must be addressed.

Before college, I worked in a bank as a teller performing all the duties that the job entailed. Though my work was no different from any of the other tellers, my pay certainly was. The reason given for this discrepancy was that the other tellers had college degrees. I suppose that could have been termed academic discrimination.

In a classic episode of the "Mary Tyler Moore" television show, Mary discovers that her predecessor (a man) had been paid considerably more for the job she now performed. In her innocently indirect way, Mary brought this to her boss's attention. Crusty and lovable Lou Grant then explained the economic facts of life to her—that a man had to be paid more because he had a family to support. Mary nodded at this logical explanation, went outside the door and paused to think. You could see the proverbial wheels turning. Then she went back into Lou's office with the observation, "Well, Mr. Grant, that would mean a man with fewer children should be paid less than a man with more children!" She got her raise, earning perhaps not as much as her predecessor, but it was a raise!

Glen, as I found out, had a wonderful sense of money in that he really didn't have a sense of it as being meaningful. He would say, when contemplating a purchase or a decision, "It's not a matter of money." How astounded I was when, one day in an art gallery, he told me to look carefully at a painting I had instantly discounted because it had a price tag of $5,000. Was this man serious? I should actually consider this painting?

As we did, it became clear this was not suitable for the space we were filling and it was not in proportion valuewise to us. A right economy or use of resources may take money into account but only as a matter of worth, not limitation. Instead, we bought a lovely tapestry that we enjoyed for many years.

So, when Glen would say, "It's not a matter of money, he was using "matter" both ways. "Money is not the subject of this discussion and it is not of consequence in the decision." He just refused to let money be the determiner of our pathway. Something higher had to be foremost in our decision making. For instance, sometimes people move to various states and even other countries just to avoid paying income tax. Likewise, investments are often made to shelter money from taxation. In many cases, money *alone* determines these actions. (Income tax laws may need to be revised and that discussion will likely go on and on, but at the basis of income tax is the concept that everyone contributes to society—to our common cause. It's a form of brotherly love, of unselfishness, and we can be grateful to participate in it.)

While some may "overvalue" (charge too much for their work or contribution to the world) there are those that "undervalue" their contribution. Finding a right balance of value is not a matter of money but of wisdom and love. We all should be rightfully blessed in our exchange of services with each other.

Wisdom is necessary in all our dealings, so that involves a right use of whatever we have at our disposal without putting any material item in a central or governing position. Money is a poor governor. Let's not elect it! Instead, *we* need to govern money as we would govern the direction our car takes or the setting on our washing machine. A "penny-pinching" attitude allows money to govern as much as does the spendthrift indulgence of a certain lifestyle. But often it's more subtle than that. The "money governing" issue will easily hide under other names. "This purchase is an answer to my prayers." Oh, that's a good one because the emphasis on money can actually clothe itself in spirituality. Or how about, "I'm simply asking for justice. I deserve nothing less." Well, it may be nothing less but it might be something considerably more, such as . . . (you guessed it) money.

Jesus made quite a startling statement in that regard when a wronged brother, one of his followers, came to him asking that justice be done. His brother wasn't sharing the inheritance with him. Seemed like a legitimate case. Did Jesus take it? No! First of all, rather than consoling the man, Jesus rebuked him, "Man, who made me a judge or a divider over you." He then turned to the others with the searing spiritual counsel, "Take heed, and beware of covetousness: for a man's life consisteth not in the abundance of the things which he possesseth" (Luke 12: 14,15). (That might make even TV's Judge Judy look lenient.)

However, this was the crux of the matter! It wasn't really a question of money at all, but another question entirely. What is our life going to consist of and what ingredients are necessary to it? Are our possessions going to determine the quality or quantity of our life? The needed "added" things (home, food, clothing) can't be the main menu or ingredients. And no, they are not the frosting on the cake or the cherry on the sundae either. Perhaps they are more like a utensil, a temporary means of eating the cake, a viable way of carrying on daily duties during our spiritual journey. The basic ingredients of our lives—the qualities of goodness, purity, unselfishness, mercy—may be found in abundance in daily living. As much as we'll allow them to be.

It really comes down to motives and goals in life, doesn't it? Working in a right direction, for the right reason, gives us the means of helping others on their journey too. But if we don't use our human resources of time, energy, money in a way that divine wisdom or intelligence directs, then things of no consequence will fritter away and deplete our time, energy and money. There's a reason this takes place. The resources we possess are not really ours (though we may have worked long and hard for them). All that we are supplied with truly comes from God and is His. So these provisions must be used for His purposes.

What then is *our* purpose? Surely, it is to discover what Love is and what Love does. In discovering that we find our true selves in the process. No identity crisis can occur while on this path. No worthlessness can plague or torment us because we are too busy reflecting divine Love. We love and cherish this gold and our golden opportunity!

Unfortunately, it's all too easy to become swept up now and then in the current concerns over money supply or retirement. But if we do, then let's just shake ourselves mentally and get on with what really matters, the work at hand. Fears, like fashions, come and go. The retirement-package mentality that exists today was not in evidence a few decades ago. But this is an economic era and concern for the future on the one hand and corporate misuse of funds on the other puts the retirement question front and center.

Of course, there is one quick way out of that—just don't retire. Wait!! I know, that's oversimplifying the situation. But surely, it would be healthier to expect increased vitality rather than decline. We can look forward to being useful, fruitful and rightly employed (though that employment may take different forms) all the days of this earthly school and beyond. For instance, news items and articles tell of individuals going to work at advanced stages of life—such as the woman, in her nineties, who puts in a full day and drives herself to work!

Have you noticed how runners will often push themselves to the limit during a race but will collapse over the finish line? If the goal is retirement, if that is our race to be run, then what does that tell us about nearing the finish line? Not a good scenario!

Women often handle "retirement" years more easily than do men because of their homemaking interests. But men, who have risen so capably and courageously to the challenge of protecting the home front, can certainly rise to the challenge that is called retirement. It's actually an advancement we are facing and not a retirement (which means pulling back). And that's another reason men may not flourish during it. It's not part of their mentality to pull back or retreat. It's truly something up "with which they will not easily put." Perhaps we can help society change the word "retirement" to "advancement."

There's always something available—work to be done, an idea that can be used, an ability to do good and these are far from worthless or useless. When used with love and wisdom, these resources (like the widow's oil) even multiply! To vacate mentally does not promote mental or physical health. To be involved in purposeful activity is healthful and fulfilling. But it is the expression of God's qualities that is the issue, not the form our work takes. So, it's of great importance not to lose our identity in any human occupation or business.

If we are in the Father's business, we'll see how truly impossible it is to retire from that. God does not retire any of His products. (They don't have a "shelf" life because He doesn't put them on the shelf to begin with.) His children are always beautiful and useful to Him. Their work is to reflect divine Life, Truth and Love. And this "work"— this joy—goes on forever!

Easy Come, Not So Easy Go

One of the most important rules for a spiritual journey, so I've found, can be contained in only one word—jettison! Remember the great escapes we've seen in films when the escapees threw all the weighty items out of a plane so it could gain altitude? Luggage went first and even plane seats were yanked from their moorings and tossed through the open door. No one stopped to paw through the luggage and select their favorite dress or shirt, you might notice. Out it all went. Yes, "jettison" is definitely the operative word here.

Quite a collection!

At the time we purchased it, the property on Palomar Mountain held thirty years of accumulated collectibles ranging from fishing-boat gear such as winches, hawser, bait tanks and an anchor to antique buggies, a cottage trailer, two vintage cars and even an old Coke™ machine. The two sea captains enjoyed collecting, it was obvious, and a family member verified this fact by describing how their family, when disposing of items, would often return with more collectibles from the mountain dump than they had deposited there. Some of the initial reluctance to sell this property clearly stemmed from the unwillingness to part with the treasures. So, Glen tore up an old shirt and went around with the owner tagging everything the man desired to keep. We even made a list headed, "Mr. T's collection."

How these items arrived at the top of the mountain in the first place was something to ponder. It might have appeared to the puzzled observer that Noah's ark had been stranded there joined by modern antiquities. (Yes, I think that's an oxymoron. They do creep in now and then, but it does carry the idea, doesn't it!) There was also the question of how the tall water tank was installed by just one man alone, the senior sea captain, who understood the power of the lever. The large steel I-beam that was left was another matter altogether. What man alone with a lever could have moved that?

Helping Mr. T. remove some of his collection was really quite an adventure. I remember when friends of ours began towing one of the old cars, with shattered windows, down a little incline of our property. Glen was steering the car, which was traveling backwards, when it suddenly began gaining on the tow vehicle. The car had no brakes so, at that point, even the field mice which had nested there began bailing out as they sensed the ship was about to sink or, in this case, about to collide. This was averted, I'm happy to say, but those watching (as concerned as we were) couldn't help laughing at the spectacle.

Redoing our mental homes.

That was only the beginning of our work to restore the property to its original parklike state and to make the little dwelling habitable. The mountain fire department joined in and held three controlled burns on the property to rid it of disintegrating debris. They enjoyed the needed practice just as much as Glen and I were enjoying burning some of the mental debris that had hung around us.

Christ Jesus gave a wonderful parable along these lines. In only one Gospel, that of Matthew (13:24-26), is found the story of the wheat and the tares. Jesus likened the kingdom of heaven to ". . . a man which sowed good seed in his field: But while men slept, his enemy came and sowed tares among the wheat, and went his way. But when the blade was sprung up, and brought forth fruit, then appeared the tares also." When the servants wanted to gather up tares, the householder prevented them, saying that they might inadvertently destroy the wheat also. They had to wait for harvest and then bind the tares into bundles to be burned and the wheat into the barn.

According to *Smith's Bible Dictionary*, the tares were a form of weed called "darnel" which could be so toxic that it might kill if ingested. Smith further explains that when the wheat is headed out, at a certain stage of development, even a child can tell the difference, though up to that point the tares might be indistinguishable from the wheat. This really describes what Glen and I had been busy with for some time. The wrong metaphysical concepts or beliefs were becoming very obvious and separate from the wheat or the actual truth of God.

Also, we tried to be careful not to pull anything out of our thinking before knowing its true character. This was a helpful lesson in many ways. For instance, we found it easy to blame ourselves for reluctance to do something when actually it turned out to be an intuitive wisdom and not reluctance at all. Be careful what you pull out before seeing the larger picture!

I think the mountain experience is interesting from the perspective of what is needed to make our own mental homes fit dwellings. Clutter has to be removed and the warmth of love installed. In the case of the little home, that meant insulation in the ceiling. We watched with admiration as my daughter, adept at gymnastics, trod the high scaffolding up into the A-frame and stapled the insulation to the beams. I watched in wonder as Glen applied pitch to the outside of the high roof to prevent more water from finding its way down the side of the chimney and into our living room. (There was no desire to repeat the night we stayed up wringing out towels, mopping up the deluge.)

I made bread and pies from scratch and applauded as Glen and one of his sons, using the antique lumber on the property, built a type of "New England bridge" covering for our newly-purchased four-wheel-drive truck. Glen and I also built a little workshop together, and many were the truckloads of brambles and various pieces from the property that I piled high for the controlled burns! Yes, there was much physical labor involved for both of us.

It's certainly true that the work we do spiritually and mentally always has to have an obvious external effect. In this case we were removing mental items we had not collected ourselves (the concepts referred to earlier that we found had crept in and received general acceptance). We were metaphysically as well as physically starting again, building on a strong foundation. Even as we outfitted the little house, we were busy correctly equipping our own mental homes for the journey we had to make and help others to make.

We took on new spiritual fuel for this journey, as answers to our many questions poured in during that time. The "little mysteries" we'd sometimes encountered in the Bible or in the writings of Mary Baker Eddy were fading out as clarity entered and concepts came into focus. This took work and so did providing fuel for the little home. With a powerful chain saw, Glen cut down dead timbers to feed the living-room fireplace and the woodstove in the bedroom. We even rented a logsplitter to make fireplace logs from the huge rounds of cedar which had been cut and left on the property.

Help for this endeavor was found in a funny article which told of a young man selling a logsplitter that could split anything. A seasoned woodsman suggested he try a certain round of wood. It couldn't be split! But there was a reason for this. You had to place the wood on the machine and split it in the direction that the tree grew and not the other way around, which was how the woodsman had fooled the salesman. Even equipped with such valuable knowledge, this was some of the most arduous labor we'd performed in our lives. (Glen and I fairly crawled back to the little house that evening). But what grand spiritual lessons were being learned all along the way. Go with the flow in the right direction, split it *with* the grain not *against* it!

It took a year and a half (half the time we lived at that residence) to completely restore the natural simplicity and uninterrupted beauty to this property. Just in case you are inclined to romanticize this experience, please note carefully the crawling back to the house, the mornings we took showers in the three by nine foot bathroom while the temperature inside was 32 degrees, then add to that the night invasion of the soldier ants and the field mice. Then you may obtain a more balanced view of life on the mountain.

Visitors would usually have either one of two reactions. After noting the lack of amenities some would quickly say, "Oh, I couldn't live like this!" Or else, having taken in the picturesque setting, others might sigh, "Oh, I wish I could live like this!" Of course, as we'd point them in the direction of the local bulletin board to find their own perfect place, a hasty retreat usually came with regrets. "It's just too far from town for me," or something of that nature. But the whole point of our living there was not for the scenery or an escape from daily pressures but to learn our spiritual lessons. It truly was a classroom.

The cyanide caper.

Ready for a little house-cleaning? It almost goes without saying that such negative states of mind as fears, insecurities and resentments should not be given space in our mental homes. Harboring hatred, for instance, is like harboring a terrorist. It makes our own mental homes vulnerable. There was an experiment years ago in which the bodily fluids produced by hate in a human being were sufficient to kill a small rodent. So, the commandment to love is not only spiritually correct but is conducive to human health. Letting in forgiveness, joy, peace and compassion are like taking that deep breath of fresh mountain air—even if getting to that higher altitude, or attitude, takes a little doing.

Now, mountain living not only provided rugged terrain but also invited rugged individualists. One such person I shall call our Mountain Man—MM for short. Rumor had it that his former life included a three-piece suit and a lawyer's briefcase (though this information remained unverified). All we knew was that MM was exceedingly strong and quite gentle, despite his appearance. With his large stature, mountain clothing, flowing beard and hair, he cut quite a figure—one that you wouldn't want to meet on a dark night. Now MM had made gates of various objects at the front of his property (at least we assumed it was his property) and took delight in the extraordinary. So it was with great alacrity that he agreed to help relieve our cluttered property of some of its accumulated treasure.

In the process of uncluttering the woodshed so we might repair it for an office, Glen told MM that he could keep whatever he found. The delightful process of discovery went smoothly until one day MM emerged from the woodshed with a can of cyanide, which appeared to have been brought into the country from our neighbor to the north. Something had to be done about this, but what? MM said he thought it was illegal. Glen just smiled and said, "I told you it was okay to keep whatever you found, so this is yours!" What a great way to pass over a problem! MM seriously accepted the cyanide duty and left. A little later we also left the property, locking the roadside gate behind us and leaving my son in the little house to do some electrical wiring.

As we passed the few stores at the top of the mountain before our descent, we noticed a police car. The customers had all been ushered out of the café and post office. They were milling around while MM, with beard flowing, was in a state of great animation in their midst. We thought this very strange until a few minutes later, we were met by another police car, siren blaring, as it raced up the mountain. Then it dawned on us. It had to do with the treasure from the woodshed. The cyanide caper was in progress.

On returning home, my son told us of the ensuing escapade. He happened to glance out the window and see nine men trooping up single-file on our property, holding handkerchiefs to their faces. He could tell MM was leading the group to the woodshed. The men entered, came out with a can of paint, and proceeded to poke it with a long stick. Finally they all left. You can imagine how puzzling all that activity must have seemed! But, there didn't appear to be any further ramifications from the incident. Mountain calm quickly returned and the cyanide caper was soon forgotten.

Invited and uninvited errors. But who created them?

And now with the exit of the cyanide, the spiritual lesson takes center stage. The fear, anger, frustration or depression that suddenly appears in our mental home may not be anything that we have intentionally brought in. Remember the young mother who invited the girl to stay for a year? That idea did not originate with the woman anymore than the cyanide originated with us.

False mental influence might be given a number of terms in Christian Science. It may be referred to as mesmerism, animal magnetism, hypnotism, mental malpractice, or aggressive mental suggestion. For instance, I recall sitting in church many years ago and suddenly feeling overwhelmed by fear. Instantly I found myself saying, under my breath, "This is not my fear!" As quickly as it came, the fear left.

There is no doubt that we reap what we sow, but what we find growing in our garden of thinking isn't necessarily something we ourselves have planted, as explained in the parable of finding tares among the wheat. ". . . An enemy hath done this," was the parable's explanation (Matthew 13:28).

Let's pick up a tennis metaphor for a moment. A ball we send across the net of life will be returned to us in the same manner we sent it out. However, stray balls may enter our court from elsewhere, sent in by mistake or on purpose. These "hits" we have not sent out—not planted and not invited. Though we have not invited the errors of thinking that we sometimes find lurking around our mental homes, we are responsible for letting them in and making them comfortable.

We are also responsible for letting in the errors that we have invited to stay with us —invited by our own reactions to people or situations. Sometimes we just "buy into" fears, anger, discouragement, disappointment, or whatever the negativity is. We allow it to be packaged and take it home with us to be displayed on our mental shelves (where it's quite obvious to others as well as ourselves). Yes, in this case we've brought the cyanide home. However—and here's a very important point—all these errors (the invited or the uninvited ones) have not been created by us. To make a mistake is not to create a mistake!

To believe ourselves to be the cause or creator of every evil we see would be incredible and unjust. That's where the popular term "it's all subjective" can be misleading. It may imply that we have created what we see, and that if we see sin then we must be sinful. Whereas in actual fact, it is what we *accept* of what we see that determines our purity or sinfulness. Jesus was sinless yet he faced multitudinous human errors or mistakes. Jesus knew that man didn't create sin but rather that sin claimed to be self-created. In John (8:44), when speaking of the sinful, devilish and murderous inclination of human nature, he said ". . . he is a liar and the father of it."

This self-made sin would then gather adherents just as the wrong math "2+2=5" might find believers. Though many might make that math mistake, no one created it. It floats in the general atmosphere only as a possibility, albeit an impossible possibility, waiting for acceptance. One may either agree or disagree with it, may be deluded by the unreal, or else agree with what is true, that 2+2=4. (Although I wanted to use other numbers, custom dictates that poor "5" be used as an example of wrong arithmetic. In the book and musical *Numberland*, in order to further the allegory, the character "5" rightfully objects to this usage.)

We do see what we entertain in our thinking. We allow for joy and goodness in our everyday lives, but this is not a creation. Man no more creates reality than he does unreality. We may either contemplate the real, agree with it and see those results . . . or else do the opposite—agree with the unreality—and see those results. But what is the point of believing the unbelievable?

When faced with the unreal, Jesus simply erased it as one would a wrong computation on the blackboard. And whether the problem was lameness, leprosy, blindness, sin or death, it had no power to resist the truth. The truth of being which Jesus knew—as to man's spiritual perfection in the likeness of God—rewrote the human symbols, with health and harmony as a result. He refused to go along with the errors on the human scene and so can we. We all have the right to refuse the cyanide!

I may possibly need it.

When I was staying with a family in Holland many years ago, the mother told me she had an intuition to buy a large drum and stock up on oil to heat their home. Soon after doing this, there was a reduced supply of available oil. Her family was well provided for during that shortage. That's a little like Joseph telling the Egyptians to stock up on food because there would be a famine in the land (Genesis 41). Wisdom does speak to us through heavenly intuitions, but this is totally different from stockpiling due to fear of what might happen. Wisdom's way is useful and fear's way is redundant and retards progress.

Have you noticed how, over the last two decades, the storage industry has suddenly sprung up? Maximize the storage in the closet (that can be helpful), add to the storage in the garage (that is bordering on the dubious), and use public storage facilities (what on earth for and when will all that stuff be used?). Of course, one could simply make their garage the storage container and keep the cars outside. Transitional storage is one thing but permanent or indecisive accumulation is quite another. What people spend on two or three years of storage could actually purchase them new furniture.

Very often, it is uncertainty regarding the future that takes up mental space and fills closets, garages and attics . . . the "I may-need-this-one-day syndrome." A friend told me her sister helped her pack a number of boxes for a move and when she moved again five years later the sister mentioned those same boxes had not been unpacked in all that time. Something is wrong with this whole picture of amassing for needs or eventualities that never occur.

Accumulation is not abundance but really representative of a poverty state of thought. It's a poor expectation that says we will not be provided for in the future unless we amass material possessions. Jesus promised that he had come for a very good reason. "I am come that they might have life, and that they might have it more abundantly" (John 10:10). He didn't promise that we would have life more *redundantly*. Redundancy is stale because it keeps rehashing or regurgitating certain states of thought or stages of life and would convince us that this past will be needed in the future. Abundant life is fresh, always ready for new spiritual adventures. It is delighted with the new prospects given each day to experience God's goodness. It glories in, but doesn't try to hoard this goodness. "It is of the Lord's mercies that we are not consumed, because his compassions fail not. They are new every morning: great is thy faithfulness" (Lamentations 3:22,23).

Various negative states of thought accumulate: Indecision, resentment, dissatisfaction, worthlessness, sorrow, covetousness, heavy-duty opinions, feeling unfulfilled, or fear for the future, all add weight to human life. They may possibly take up space on the body as extra weight, or take up storage space elsewhere. What do we do with these states of thinking? We jettison them. Baggage (mental and physical) needs to be released. It weighs us down.

I think Paul had the best advice for anyone wanting to make spiritual progress and take off the earth weights (wherever they appear) in the process, ". . . let us lay aside every weight, and the sin which doth so easily beset us, and let us run with patience the race that is set before us" (Hebrews 12:1). If we want to have dominion over time and space, we'll rid ourselves of the clutter. In the process we may even unearth precious talents and abilities.

I love the lasting lessons of simplicity learned early from my mother who could pack to go anywhere in about half an hour. She believed in and practiced what I would call an elegant simplicity (a term used by a physicist to describe the universe). Though beautiful in appearance as well as in character, she had no yearning for pampering or luxury items, so her clothes were few but in good taste. She told me that if there was a dress in my closet that I couldn't wear, it was taking the place of something I could wear. And she loved order. There was no clutter in her life. My parents' rule of thumb was that something had to be beautiful and useful or out it went! Of course a right amount of decorating—bringing joy and color into the home—was considered useful.

The little house on the mountain provided wonderful opportunities to practice simplicity. It was really enjoyable to see just how simply one could live without practicing false frugality. What a freedom that was! Years later, I recall hearing a man on television say he actually felt relieved when his house, with all his possessions, burned down. Perhaps he had an overpacked garage.

In today's society, it takes constant work to stay ahead of the clutter! But, if our home is clogged up what does that say about our thinking and our lives? Is there any room for a free flowing of ideas? Actually, one's home is an excellent place to discover just what we do have in our thinking—and it's a great place to shop for another family, as can be seen by the following.

A young woman I knew with a little nine-year old daughter was a hard-working single mother with not a lot of extras in her life. So, when a neighbor held an estate sale I invited her over. The neighbor told my friend she could take any of the canned food items and kitchen cleaners, paper towels, etc. for only $10. We loaded baskets, filled as full as we could get them, into the trunk of her small car. When she arrived home, her daughter watched as her mother unpacked the "goodies." The child with eyes wide exclaimed, "Oh, Mama, we're rich!"

If some cleaning equipment, paper towels and cans of tuna can bring this much joy to a child just think of what shopping in our closets and cabinets for another family could do! It's a double blessing. It adds to one while subtracting clutter from another. What a perfect match! And there are many organizations ready to receive these donations and make the match for us. I remember a man who, after donating several carloads of accumulation, was able to have the first good night's sleep he'd had in six weeks!

The trend today seems to be a mix of wanting simplicity, yet building complexity, which may run the gamut from labor-saving machines (like computers) to housing tracts. A friend recently told me that a new housing development in her neighboring community was advertising homes with eleven bedrooms. Eleven bedrooms! Perhaps they were expecting a football team to occupy it.

Spirituality really isn't such a mystery. In fact, it's almost too practical. If it were mysterious then we could merely believe in it and not have to practice it. So, the question constantly, daily recurs: Are we trusting in matter, in material things, or are we trusting in things of the Spirit, in spiritual things? And our lives daily answer this question from the small to the large details.

Biting into the apple of worldly wisdom—wealth and accumulation—won't make us wise or truly rich, but could rob us of the "simplicity that is in Christ" as Paul feared might happen (II Corinthians 11:3). We even may find that simplicity and freedom from debt are inextricably linked together. Going into debt is trusting the future to take care of the excesses of today. Far better to live as simply as possible and in the present moment. There are sufficient problems to solve today, without trusting in or fearing for the future. Jesus' sublimely simple counsel says it all, "Take therefore no thought for the morrow: for the morrow shall take thought for the things of itself. Sufficient unto the day is the evil thereof" (Matthew 6:34). Good can only happen in the "forever now." There is no other time for it to take place.

Let the good times roll!

But it's not always the future that gives us problems. Often it's the past. But the good (or bad) of the past can't compete with the good of the present time. For instance, it's hard to live on the memory of a great meal we had last week. Oh, but we do try!

Have you ever dragged around old joys, like vintage videos, hoping for a rerun? My ice skates took up quite a bit of room (I have long feet) in our luggage but I dragged them along as my family moved from country to country during my teens. Years later, I yearned for the good old times skating. "If I just had a skating rink near me how happy I would be!"

Then one was built only eight blocks away. Happy days were here again, or so I thought as a friend and I took our children skating. What an eye-opener! The music was all wrong, the teenage boys were no longer interesting to me and the ice was hard and cold. I had enjoyed the activity in another context, that of my high-school days, and this context couldn't be repeated. I never returned to that ice-rink. And it's very possible that a friend of mine is not going to try another rerun of her past joys, either.

Kathy, as we shall call her, had a lingering longing (as strange as this may sound) to do some household chores. Well, to her they were not simply chores but homemaking. Her work demanded that she be at the telephone a good part of the day, but she was a natural at making her home lovely. However, happy little homemaker memories were beginning to fade under the pressure of daily demands. That is why, when it came time to seal the large tiles on her floor inside and out on the patio she elected to do it herself. It should be fun and she relished the idea. (I told you this was rather strange, and it gets even better.)

So Kathy went off to rent a stripping machine to clean the tiles before sealing them. She didn't wonder when the man put a rather cumbersome contraption into her car. Nor did she give it much thought when her husband had to help her get it out. He, by the way, was firmly convinced they should hire someone to do the job, so he was keeping "hands off" the project. Kathy cheerfully arranged all her equipment that night ready for the next day's adventure. She had knee pads, bucket, stripping liquid and so forth.

I called late the next day to find out how it all went and this was, in essence, the conversation.

How are you doing? Is it all finished?

No, I'm down on my knees trying to strip the floor.

You're trying to strip the floor? What about the machine?

Well, when I plugged it in, the machine was so heavy that it just took off on its own and ran all over the balcony, banging into walls and everything. I couldn't control it.

Oh, that's too bad. Didn't your husband help?

Well, yes, he did get it under control but then it blew a fuse.

Couldn't you reset the fuse?

We did and it blew every time. Then we couldn't start the machine again.

Oh, so you couldn't use the machine after all?

Right! That's why I'm on my knees. But they're getting very red.

How come your knees are getting red?

It's because the plastic baggies slipped off.

Plastic baggies? What about the knee pads?

I couldn't use them. They were wet.

Why were they wet?

They were in the bucket outside overnight.

Yes, and ?

Well, it rained last night!

Oh, I see.

That's why my knees are red and I haven't made much progress.

This wasn't so much fun, then?

Not that you could notice!

We were, of course, both laughing at this juncture. In Kathy's case, past pleasure and practical present didn't match up.

To test yearnings, it might be helpful to find out whether it was the activity itself or the activity within a certain context that was appealing. If the activity can be performed in various contexts (old movies of composers writing on restaurant tablecloths in Vienna come to mind), then perhaps the music, art or skating is being propelled by something more than a certain place, a certain time or a certain context, because it can stand on its own.

Of course, it's not simply the context of past pleasures that we hold onto, but it is often the form of past duties that would hold us captive. If one were starting fresh, what is the decision that would be made today? is a good question. I suggested this to someone who was part of a group that felt burdened by upkeep of their facilities. Though suitable for them in the past, these facilities were more than needed at the present moment, but the group continued in the same manner, as though the past were present. I suggested they might like to think of it in these terms: If all their resources were liquid, what would they do with them today? Would they buy those same facilities if they were for sale?

Not long after that conversation, I saw part of a TV program in which Suze Orman, a well-known financial expert, suggested that exact same procedure for evaluating stocks. If your funds were liquid would you buy into that stock today? She said if you wouldn't, then it was time to sell the stock. She humorously described how hard it is to drive forward by looking in the rearview mirror all the time. She said you can't be benefited if you keep looking back at the past performance of the stock, hoping it will return to its former position of value.

This is good advice for many areas of life. For instance, we are not trying to return to former positions of good health or plentiful supply; rather, we desire to experience the God-given health and provision that are present right here and now. All of us want to progress in one way or another. We'd like to get ahead, go ahead, look ahead, forge ahead, plough ahead, full-steam ahead. No one wants to slide backwards, especially if we're hoping to make good progress on our spiritual journey.

How can we be fit for and ready to receive spiritual good, the health and harmony that is both here and ahead of us, if we keep on looking backwards? Jesus told us that in just one clear statement, ". . . No man, having put his hand to the plough, and looking back, is fit for the kingdom of God" (Luke 9:62).

It was just a little car.

Perhaps some of the hardest things to let go of are those with a sentimental attachment. I've wondered if those who have kept many family mementoes will one day meet their mother, for instance, and tell her, "I kept all those memories of you!" and she will reply, "You mean to say, you cluttered up *your* life with *my* life!" That's a possible hereafter conversation. True or not, there is a great need for simplicity.   So, I'm eager to advise others to "let it all go." Then it came to selling "Little Car."

Now as you may have surmised, Glen and I were not collectors. We even disposed of a large portion of our worldly goods when we went up to the small house on the mountain. This was certainly true when, some years later, we moved to Hawaii for a couple of years. Everything we owned at that point was in suitcases that fit into our little white hatchback FX 16 Toyota. (By the way, that particular model had a sports engine and was very peppy despite its demure and utilitarian appearance.)

Glen and I both felt glad about being able to relinquish material possessions, but I neglected to notice there was one thing that still remained—the container for the basic necessities—"Little Car" as we affectionately called it.

Glen and I had purchased the car new in 1986. When Glen passed on in 1993, I still chugged along in . . .well, you know its name. I heard Toyotas went forever, so I was keeping it up to the best of my ability and trusted in that prediction. I think the wise ones who declared this should have added: "It goes forever if you happen to be a good mechanic."

The third time the air-conditioning went out seemed like a bridge too far, especially as I had to do a good amount of summertime traveling at that time. On praying about this, it felt right to visit the local Toyota dealer while Little Car was in the garage (a new air-conditioning unit was not forthcoming as sixteen-year-old cars are either too hard to outfit or else the search was not frantic enough).

It was the last day of July (which I later learned is one of the best times to go car shopping). So I came out with a two-year-old Corolla, their lead item, which also just happened to be in one of my favorite car colors—a cranberry red.

Now the jockeying began because my parking spaces are front-to-back not side-by-side. It became increasingly obvious that the time for Little Car was past, but I felt this strange pull about letting it go. One night, while chastising myself for this emotion, I said out loud these words, "Well, I know what Glen would say if he were here!" Immediately, I heard the mental response, "Keep it, honey. If it makes you feel better, keep it!"

You can imagine how startled I felt and for three reasons. First of all, I was sure Glen would tell me to get over it and get on with it. Secondly, I don't talk to myself in those endearing terms. Thirdly, I don't believe in spiritualism or that type of communication with those gone on.

But then I realized that divine Love was telling me what Glen would really say to me in this situation. I was basing my judgment on what we had done, or would do, together. Furthermore, it was clear that if the situation had been reversed—if he had been here and feeling pulled about letting the car go, I would have said to him, "Keep it, honey. If it makes you feel better, keep it!"

The next morning I sold Little Car. I was even able to see it drive away without a tear or an emotional wrench. The answer was immediate. The trap was off and the love of God so complete that it removed the sentiment, giving me a deeper sense of Glen's loving-kindness while freeing me to go ahead. The sentimental temptation to hold on to that little car was simply a temptation to believe in death. But how can we progress in our journey to the understanding of eternal Life while we hold on to outdated beliefs in death? We can't be dead to Life. No wonder Christ Jesus said, ". . . Follow me; and let the dead bury their dead" (Matthew 8:22).

The two thieves crucified on either side of Jesus represent, to me, the past and the future and are a painful reminder not to place our hopes there. Past or future certainly are robbers. The now of the Christ is the only moment we have available and it is never ending. We truly live in the forever now and always at the point of high noon (if we think of that as the point of perfection).

"The spirit of aloha."

Living love in the present moment might well be described as "the spirit of aloha." This Hawaiian word means "love" and is used both as a greeting and as a farewell. "Hello," "Goodbye," and "I love you," is how it was first explained to me. Since then, I've often heard the phrase "much aloha" implying warmth, friendliness and love.

When Glen and I lived in Hawaii (in the non-tourist parts of it), we were impressed with the kindness and patience of the people. If one held up traffic to talk to a passerby, the car behind waited patiently. If one paused to chat with a store clerk, the next customer was more likely to join in (with kindly interest) than to look at their watch.

Since then, I've watched for opportunities to practice this. When in the process of writing this chapter, I left my intended purchases at a jewelry counter to buy a card and when I returned another woman was being waited on. She kindly offered to let me go ahead. Instead, I urged her to make her selection and joined in the conversation about it. When she later caught sight of me in the parking lot, she hailed me as she would an old friend, with warmth and smiles. Yes, Hawaii was our "kindness" and "gentleness" classroom, and the beauty of those lessons surpassed even the beauty of the Islands.

To experience how divine Love meets our daily needs, it is imperative to live with and in that "spirit of aloha." As it permeates our greetings and our meetings we find out just how present Love is. What a difference such qualities as kindness, patience, and gentleness could make to today's busy world!

One day, a family member called and wished me "Good noon," because it happened to be right at that moment she called. In thinking about it, this is spiritually accurate. We are not *before* or *after* noon, or any point in time, for our spiritual nature is always at the point of perfection that God knows. Finding and understanding this point of perfection is our journey home.

Wishing someone "Good noon" is rather like saying "aloha." It could mean "Hello," "Goodbye," or "I acknowledge and love the beautiful spiritual being that you indeed are." The present is truly a wonderful gift!

Rough Company? It ain't Necessarily So

When Jesus urged "Follow me" he was not advocating an armchair activity or a spectator sport. His command requires "much aloha," much active participation. It entails loving God and our brother man in increasingly deeper and more spiritual ways. It means seeing more of reality and not judging falsely, that is, by the appearance. So, I'd like to share with you some greetings and farewells along these lines of aloha.

Prayer on the El.

Before I met Glen he lived in Chicago and often traveled on the elevated railway (the El) to his office. One day, only Glen and a woman were in the railway car as the train sped along. The peace was suddenly shattered as a rock came hurtling through the window. Glass showered the two occupants and the woman began screaming hysterically. Glen asked if she was alright. As she continued to scream, he fairly shouted, "Are you alright?" She quieted somewhat and replied, "Yes. Yes, I'm okay."

"Then let's give our attention to the frustration that threw that rock. Let's pray for that individual," Glen suggested. After a few moments of prayerful silence, the woman turned to him and asked, "What church do you attend? I'm looking for a Sunday School for my children." How wonderful that what had the potential of being a rough experience turned into a blessing for all. The individual who threw the rock was the beneficiary of sincere prayers; a woman had her question answered in a very quiet but telling way, and Glen, who loved to share good, was given an opportunity to do just that.

Finding freedom in prison.

Glen had many opportunities to share his love of God when serving on the Christian Science Board of Lectureship for his lecture tours took him across the United States, Canada, and to Europe. He willingly accepted invitations to lecture in prisons, even maximum-security prisons where the lecturer had to undergo a strip search before being allowed to enter. He told me how spiritually hungry were the individuals he encountered in these facilities. As one man told him after a lecture, "It was worth coming to prison, to learn about God."

One lecture took place on a rainy afternoon. The room filled with inmates who did not particularly want to attend but simply hoped to stay dry. As Glen began lecturing, one noisy section made its presence felt by making catcalls, heckling and generally carrying on in a disruptive manner. One man was evidently the ring leader of the group and so it was to him that Glen directed this attention grabber: "Hey, you there! There's one difference between you and me!" "Yeah, and what's that?" was the jeering reply amidst laughter from his buddies. Glen anwered, "Well, in one hour I get to leave here and you don't. Do you want to hear about that difference?"

I think in the vernacular of today that might be termed a "gutsy move." Maybe it appeared that way to the inmate or else it just totally intrigued him because he motioned to his cohorts with one sweep of the hand and said, "Hey, you guys, knock it off!" And they did. For the remainder of the hour it was absolutely quiet as the lecture was given. Those inmates had escaped the rain into some spiritual sunshine and, hopefully, they could feel it.

In another instance, it was quite apparent just how much the lecture meant to one inmate. When Glen finished, a little line formed as the inmates wanted to have a few words with the lecturer. But as the line moved slowly, one man was being summoned over the loud speaker. "Prisoner number . . . report to . . . ." The prisoner stayed in line as the summons was repeated. Before he could reach Glen, a couple of guards appeared and escorted him away. Another prisoner remarked that his infraction would cost that man a couple of days in solitary confinement.

Again, it's hard to judge by appearances. What seemed to be a sad thing in that he didn't reach Glen was perhaps a wonderful provision of good for that inmate. He was given two whole days alone during which he could quietly think over what he'd heard.

As moral sensibility increases, the criminal suffers for his crime. He becomes his own punishment and punisher. But there is a way out and it's called reformation. The best work of prisons is surely not punishment but reformation. For instance, a man who was serving two consecutive life sentences for murder was being considered for parole because, according to the prison authorities, he was no longer the same man who committed those crimes. He had been entirely rehabilitated. He was a new man.

Just how long was that sentence?

Religion, usually supposed to be suffused with love, is less loving than our judicial system if it forever damns a sinner or criminal. At least the judicial system carries its penalty no farther than this world, even when imposing two or three life sentences on a murderer. The verdict, given on behalf of religion, that an individual will "burn in hell forever" does not take into account the higher law of divine Love. That fiery verdict is perhaps based on one statement of "everlasting punishment" found in the New Testament. In fact "punishment" is mentioned only that one time in all of the four Gospels (Matthew 25:46), and only 9 times total in all of the New Testament, while "love" appears about 190 times.

This is where it helps to look at everything said on the subject of punishment, the context in which it appears, and the overriding message of the Gospels. The greater part of Scripture consistently testifies to the everlasting kindness and love of God. "The Lord hath appeared of old unto me, saying, Yea, I have loved thee with an everlasting love: therefore with lovingkindness have I drawn thee" (Jeremiah 31:3). So might not the phrase "everlasting punishment" simply be a warning that the punishment lasts as long as the sin?

God's love for man never ends, but sin comes to an end. As long as we are off the right road and out in the brambles, we get scratched and bruised. That particular punishment is everlasting, or lasting as long as the wrong direction. On the right road, there is no self-punishment for sin. Surely the best forgiveness of sin is to wipe it out. The third tenet of Christian Science is simply that: "We acknowledge God's forgiveness of sin in the destruction of sin and the spiritual understanding that casts out evil as unreal. But the belief in sin is punished so long as the belief lasts" (*Science and Health*, p. 497).

It's a human not a divine verdict that says, "You have one chance to perform well and it's in this lifetime only and if you blow it, that's it!" Last Chance Saloon! That's enough to drive someone to drink (and it probably has).

Jesus could not have possibly come to save us *in this world only*, either from sin or sickness—or even death, for that matter. That's what Paul told the Corinthians, "If in this life only we have hope in Christ, we are of all men most miserable" (I Corinthians 15:19). The fact that Jesus demonstrated there is no death and that life continues should be enough to prove that we are given more opportunity hereafter to work out the problem of being. Every step of the way our Principle, our heavenly Parent, loves and guides us to the perfect solution. A child isn't allowed only elementary school in which to learn everything needed for graduation from college. There's even a remedial class in college—in English for instance—and students who are deficient in that subject must remedy their failings before continuing with higher education.

Science and Health explains that Jesus proved (because one's physical condition is unchanged after death) that there is "a probationary and progressive state beyond the grave" (p. 46). People who have died in the commission of a crime, been executed, or simply died an unrepentant sinner will have to do their remedial work hereafter.

That's why capital punishment only results in pushing people out of this world (because they deserve it or the jails are crowded) into another system, where other workers might have to deal with the criminal and their problems. I don't think those beyond here would thank us for that. Dying, or rather passing on to the next experience, is not a lasting solution for anything. Surely it would be better to work on reformation, and endeavor to make our U-turns, here and now.

Two gentlemen of Chicago.

It was during his lecturing days that Glen had another meaningful encounter on the El. He was sitting beside a man who was staring at his heavily-bandaged hands. Glen noticed and felt he should say something spiritually reassuring to the injured man. Suddenly an intuition came not to speak to that man, but to another man who was standing beside them holding onto the strap of the train. This man smoked a cigarette while he glared at those around him. Wanting to be obedient to the angel message, Glen looked for an opener. There was a "no smoking" sign close by so Glen mentioned that fact in a kindly manner and pointed to the sign.

The man to whom Glen spoke was very large, burly and a rather rough-looking individual. However, he nodded and put his cigarette out. But a moment later he apparently rethought his conformity to the law and lit another cigarette. What's more, he defiantly puffed smoke in Glen's face. Glen continued to smile, shrugged and murmured, "It's okay, no big deal." At the next stop, the man with bandaged hands left the train, leaving the seat available for Glen's new acquaintance.

The burly man sat down next to Glen, glared at him again, but in a moment put out his cigarette, and turned to Glen with the comment, "It's good that two men can have a difference of opinion and settle it like gentlemen." Glen agreed and they began to talk. When asked what he did, Glen didn't simply reply that he gave lectures, but for some reason (intuition again no doubt) said he gave lectures in prisons.

The man became very interested and asked which ones. As Glen reeled them off, the man would interject now and then with, "Oh, yes, I've been there." They had something in common! They'd both been in the same prisons—under different arrangements, of course. Glen was then able to share with the man what sinless, spiritual selfhood is all about and the man's face shone with joy. He took Glen's hand and shook it so gratefully as he left the train.

ROUGH COMPANY? IT AIN'T NECESSARILY SO

It's all too easy to get carried away with our own plans for doing good, or to judge erroneously as to which individual one should help.   The clear need for heavenly guidance in our daily lives inspired me to write a poem about this incident on the El.

Your plan, dear Father

What would You have me do today,
What would You have me say?
Where would You have me go today,
For what would You have me pray?

I have a list of things to do
I wrote down every one,
Duties that I must perform
And errands to be run.

But what would You have me do today,
What does Your list include?
I long to know what Love has planned
And what it does exclude.

I thought of what my dear one did
When traveling on the El,
He yearned so much to share what's good,
He had the truth to tell.

Beside him sat an injured man,
At bandaged hands he stared.
Beside him stood a rugged man;
At those around he glared.

Before my dear one could utter a word
To comfort the bandaged one,
An angel thought quickly came,
"Not him! Speak to the other one."

At the very next stop the first man left,
The other now sat beside.
He glared at my dear one once again,
Then in him he did confide.

"I've been in a number of prisons," he said,
"But now I've been let out."
"Really? I've talked in a number of prisons
And sometimes I had to shout."

They compared the list of prisons,
Some of them were the same,
Then my dear one said he recognized him
Though he didn't know his name.

He explained he knew that in actual truth
His companion was God's own child;
And as he shared these beautiful thoughts
The man became meek and mild.

They parted with such friendly smiles,
The man offered a firm handshake.
His demeanor showed a new uprightness,
He had a new path to take.

It is Love that leads us to comfort those
Whose wounds we cannot see,
To bind them in the goodness of God
And help them to be free.

So, again I ask, more meekly now,
Your perfect plan to know.
What would *You* have me do today,
And where would *You* have me go?

"Get me an attorney!"

My list of duties over these last years has included frequent trips to the post office. It was on one such errand, while turning the corner into the parking lot, that I became aware of a commotion taking place. A man, shouting obscenities, was being pinned against the wall of a store by another man. The police were arriving and I hurried on my way into the post office past the hubbub. On leaving, I found this man sitting in the back of a police car. He was still ranting and raving and, as I passed by, he shouted to me, "Hey, miss, get me an attorney!"

Get him an attorney? I didn't think so! But as I pondered it on the way to my car, it seemed to me the best attorney I could give him was an understanding of the truth of being as found in the Bible and the Christian Science textbook. That was an attorney that could argue his case for him. Then the thought came to give him a copy of *The Ultimate Freedom* that I had in the car.

My dad's account of his wartime imprisonment, though under different circumstances, has been and is such a beacon of light to those in prisons. One prison librarian told me it was so popular he couldn't keep it on the shelves (it being constantly checked out, not pirated) even though he had a number of donated copies available. An inmate in a Texas prison sent me a card one Christmas thanking me for publishing the book, saying it was, "a real contribution to mental freedom."

To give the man in the police car this book seemed like a good idea, but it appeared as though they would leave at any moment as the engine was running. I hesitatingly went and picked up the book. As I returned, they were still there—the two policemen in the front seat and the noisy passenger in back. How should I go about this? A woman was talking with another policeman to the side of the car, so I asked him, "Please, could you let him have this book? It will help him think in a better way." He took a look at the book, front and back, then handed it through the window to a policeman, saying, "Give him this!"

Suddenly there was silence in that car and, as it drove slowly away, I could see the policemen both looking at the book and the man in the back, peering between them to see what he was going to be given. Interestingly, I overhead the woman asking the policeman I'd spoken to if he had made the arrest. He said, "Oh, no. I'm a detective." It appeared that I had probably given the book to the only one who had the authority to hand it in to the police car.

The spiritual intuitions or angel messages that come to us always have a means by which we can carry out the assignment. Mere human goodness on its own can run out of steam, can lose heart, lose hope. So it's important that goodness be on a higher level. If goodness pivots on God first, then on the divine law of loving one's neighbor—if it claims nothing for itself but gives all glory to the Principle of being, God, good—it is able to maintain a stronger course because it is connected to its heavenly source.

Each one of us needs the good connection—the connection to what is good and lasting. Many of the problems today with juveniles (as well as with adults) are said to arise from lack of a meaningful connection with something good in their lives. To bring the spiritually real into our lives was Jesus' mission. Over and over again, he showed that unmistakable link to God. I believe it was this type of connection that was made one day by a man sitting on the ground in front of the post office.

"Maybe that's the answer!"

A poorly dressed man was shaking a tin cup and asking for money from passersby. I was careful about giving money and usually tried to give food and "food for thought" instead. This time I needed no excuse and told him that I had just emptied my purse of all its change. But on entering the post office the thought came to me strongly, "Give him something." So on leaving, I mentioned that I might have a couple of quarters in the car.

As I scooped them up, I took with me a copy of the *Christian Science Sentinel*. I handed the money to the man and then the magazine, saying, "This will do you more good than money ever could." I was leaning down to talk with him and could smell liquor on his breath, but it seemed so irrelevant that it could have been root beer I was smelling.

He looked at the magazine then said, "In '76 I thought I could make a difference," and a tear rolled down his cheek. "You still can," I assured him, but he passed off my comment by motioning with his cane towards one leg that had evidence of some problem (the skin was all discolored). So I told him, "You can be healed," and showed him the testimonies of healing in back of the *Sentinel*. He looked at them and then said slowly, "Christian Science. Well, maybe that's the answer." Then he quickly added, as though remembering something important on this very subject, "God gave me my brain and my math." As I left, I reassured him that he could still use both.

The next day as I approached the post office there he was again on the ground and I wondered what more I could possibly say to him. As I drew near I noticed his cup sitting beside him while he was totally engrossed in working on a crossword puzzle. He never looked up and was still busy when I left. Well, he was definitely using his intelligence (his brain, as he put it).

A week or so later I glimpsed him passing in front of the post office holding his cane high above his head in a rather triumphant manner as he walked quickly with long, confident strides. That was the last I saw of him. Rough company? It ain't necessarily so.

Serving Wins the Game! It's a Love Match

It is just about impossible to beat someone with a great serve. That's true in tennis and it's true in life. There are tennis players who can rocket a ball at more than one hundred miles an hour across the net, and who has a chance of returning that! Someone with a powerful serve can ace each shot and the game ends up as a "love match," meaning the other player wins no points at all. In thinking about our form of service to each other and to humanity in general, we may well ask the question: How can we make it a real love match, where everyone wins and is benefited?

A powerful serve.

Christ Jesus served so well. He served God and mankind without a fault and it may be fair to draw the parallel, in a most respectful manner, and say that he aced every serve. But in this love match everyone won. Those were and are the rules of the game. Yes, serving does win the game and it is a love match! Jesus had told his followers that he came not to be ministered unto but to minister to others. He came not to be served but to serve. He even washed the disciples' feet and brought home the lesson to them: "If I then, your Lord and Master, have washed your feet; ye also ought to wash one another's feet" (John 13:14).

The world does not necessarily value those in service positions. They are usually paid less and admired less. I met a young man, incredibly polite and helpful, in an office supply store who had come to this country from the Philippines with his wife and eight-year-old son. Previously, he'd held a position in a university where he aided students. It was evidently a good job but now he was, quite cheerfully, starting all over again.

The spirit of cheerful serving is a wonderful quality to possess. It gives joy to the person being served and joy to the helper. Nothing can quite replace this spirit. We can't delegate our spiritual progress to another and we can't delegate serving. All we can do is pray for the opportunity to be of service and we'll receive that opportunity along with directions and a basic instruction about pushing.

Which way are we pushing?

In removing the accumulation from our mountain home, Glen and I faced the daunting task of removing a very old water heater, seeming to weigh a ton, that leaned casually against the house next to the front door. A couple of friends offered to help Glen and the three men set their shoulders to the task, intending to make quick work of the matter. However, after a minute or two of fruitless pushing they all stood back, mopping their brows. It was a strange thing to watch for it appeared as though they had met their match in this cumbersome relic. However, the three of them set to it again with greater effort, but with the same result, until one of them gasped, "Say, guys, which way are you pushing?" Yes, they were pushing *against* not *with* each other!

How smoothly our journey would flow if we all pushed *with* instead of *against* each other. It doesn't take much effort to make an appointment at someone else's convenience if we're able to do it. It doesn't cost a thing to open a door, smile a smile or help locate a missing object. Just that one concept alone of pushing with each other can change a grueling work day into a pleasant experience. Ask someone at your office to try this experiment with you and see the results. Find ways to push together—to make the path easier for each other. Perhaps we should hang a placard at home or at work, "This is a **push-with-each-other** environment."

A little service, please!

Pushing *with* each other makes everyone's journey go more smoothly and quickly because love greases the runway. Besides, it's a privilege to show another that they too are cared for and loved.

Does this mean we accept everything another wants to do and in their own good time? No, obviously not, and we are always free to make other choices if it appears as though our kindness is being taken advantage of. However, it is still better to err on the side of being taken advantage of than to harm another.

Resisting sloppy or tardy work may be necessary but even then *how* we resist is the question. Glen told of a car repair which almost ended in a fist fight after he had complained to the mechanic's boss. I'll excerpt this from his lecture, "Let Your Basis Be Love."

"I'd taken my car to have a minor adjustment. The mechanic told me to come back in an hour to pick up. I did. The car hadn't been touched. I went back a second time and still no car.

249

I was a bit irritated. Well, maybe more than a bit! I called the mechanic's boss and registered my complaint—and my irritation, too.

"Now, about this time, I also started to recognize I hadn't been loving at all in my attitude. Regardless of the apparent inconvenience, I couldn't find any real peace until I got my thinking straight. So I put aside the irritation and inconvenience and thought of all the examples of divine Love I could, until I began to feel God's boundless love flooding my consciousness.

"In this much more enlightened frame of thinking, I went back to pick up my car. Apparently the mechanic's boss had relayed my remarks to him. As I came into the station, the mechanic came bursting out through the door. His face livid with rage. He reached out to grab me by the collar. His fist was clenched. And he started to swing! But he stopped right in midair. His expression changed. His arms dropped to his sides and he turned and went back in the filling station. I can't tell you the gratitude that welled up in me as I recognized the Love I'd been praying to. Why, the power of this Love had extended and included him.

"He came out a few minutes later smiling—and my car was now adjusted. He apparently had no recall of his former anger at all. Courtesy, even friendliness had replaced his anger. You see, as I related to divine Love as God, the power of God's love was reflected in my own experience."

Serving on what basis?

At the same time that Glen was having his learning experiences, halfway across the country I was learning my own lessons regarding serving.

There was a time when family needs of both close and extended members were rather pressing. Added to that were the calls for spiritual help that came constantly. During this period, I found myself experiencing pain in one shoulder and it didn't lessen despite my metaphysical efforts. Then it became clear to me that I had the "proverbial chip on my shoulder" in that I was feeling put upon. I really loved helping and wanted to do it, but at the same time the idea of being responsible for all this seemed a bit much.

Now, one can't always tie things up as neatly as that. It would be grossly unfair to say that everyone with a painful shoulder is resentful about a situation. In my case, it just happened to be accurate and when I released the burden of how much I thought I was doing, the pain ceased. The serving has to be unselfish.

Since that time, I've come to see the difference between having rightful responsibilities and duties or taking on false responsibility for another. We do have a brotherly duty to love and care for others. Duty, performed unselfishly, is not a heavy load but an opportunity. However, responsibility for another's life or happiness is a burden and a false one. Each individual is responsible for their own decisions regarding life and happiness.

Years ago a woman came to me with a difficult situation. She was having to take a widow, who couldn't drive, on regular trips to the supermarket. This had gone on for a whole year and she wondered was there any end in sight. This type of situation made me think in terms of an equation:

A need + my ability to fill it + my willingness to do it = doing it.

There's only one problem. This is a human equation and God does not appear anywhere in it. Remember the old game "Mother may I?" in which children needed to ask that question before enacting something? That's still valid. The first love is in first place for a good reason, and we can't make the second love for our neighbor primary over our love for God, the divine Mind, which is the intelligence of our universe. Unless we begin by listening to this Mind for directions, we won't know whom to help, how to help or when to help.

As Glen said, "we can't plan good enough." Remember, too, his experience on the El when told to "speak to the other one." That woman helping the widow might have been led by God to continue what she was doing for awhile or perhaps help her friend find a more permanent solution—a driver's license or a home close to a market. Wondering what people think (or will think) about our actions shows we are not going to God first. Our duty is first to God and then to man. This is wisdom's way.

Women, in particular, feel accused in these areas so it's really helpful to make that distinction of listening to God before acting. The story of Adam and Eve points up very clearly the various problems mortal men and women may encounter. Eve was considered responsible for enticing Adam to eat the forbidden fruit (as though he had no choice in the matter) and, of course, she was also formed to serve Adam (be a good helpmeet). She had better make sure everything went smoothly!

Of course, there wasn't a great scenario on Adam's side, either. He had the responsibility of constant toil—working by the sweat of the brow—to provide necessities. And in the course of this exhilarating endeavor, he may need to carry a spear in one hand to defend his property, and to chase off the business competition, too.

This material view of life, firmly planted on the belief that man is made from dust, from matter, does have its problems for both men and women. The burdens of separate duties may have shifted in recent times but the basis of the human scene is what needs to shift. If it doesn't, the changing patterns of duty might simply fall into the category of "rearranging the deck chairs on the Titanic." The material, mortal vessel of life is always headed towards the iceberg.

The question of evolution versus creation science can be solved by replying that the question is wrong, because both sides are actually arguing on the same side of the case. They are both arguing for a material view of life. That's a little like having two prosecuting attorneys try a case, with no defense attorney present. Neither attorney is in favor of the defendants. How did the perpetrators arrive at the scene of the crime? One attorney argues, "I think they got here by this road," and then comes the rebuttal, "That's not correct; they took another route entirely." No matter, because in the final analysis, they are all guilty of mortality, and will be sentenced accordingly.

Now these are very deep and sincere questions, so I don't mean to make light of them—but only to present them in a different light. Changing the context can be illuminating. And that's really what we are talking about, isn't it? We need to change the context in which we view life.

The power of the universe is spiritual, not material. God is Spirit, not matter. And Spirit doesn't push us into the mortality pool from which we hope to be fished out at a later date, possibly hereafter. No matter how we think we arrived in a material condition, the fact remains that a spiritual idea can't become material and the delusional mortal dream saying that is possible must cease. So, what will be our reality? is a better question. If we start from a spiritual home base we can run the bases and make a spiritual home run.

Now, let's go to another side of serving for a moment. Serving well and unselfishly on our home run journey also includes freedom from needless curiosity (that was Eve's problem). When ushering at an event, I didn't feel very well so I asked another usher to exchange places with me. (She was in a position behind the podium, hidden from public view, while I was stationed at the front door.)

On hearing this request, she immediately replied, "Yes, of course." She didn't ask why and, I could see by her face, she didn't even *wonder* why; she simply exchanged places. I don't recall to this day what the problem was, but I have never forgotten that woman's readiness to serve without curiosity.

Another kind act of serving remains in memory. When my little family and I moved to a new home we were invited by the neighbors to come over for dinner. However, by the end of the day, we were all tired and dirty and just didn't want to go out. So I asked my new neighbor if it would be at all possible for us to eat what she had so lovingly prepared in our own home. She happily and immediately packed up all the goodies, including the ice cream, and we quietly and very gratefully ate in the privacy of our home.

What unselfishness was demonstrated in that willingness because the neighbor couldn't hear our comments of appreciation as we ate the dinner nor could we remark on the loveliness of her home. This still remains, to me, a wonderful example of meeting another's need without feeding our own self satisfaction. Unselfish service with a smile is beautiful and truly memorable.

A new definition of prettiness.

Beauty and kindness do seem to be closely related as can be seen by the following incident. A friend of mine had trouble with her car and it needed to be towed into the repair shop, which at that time was swamped with work, as the man explained to her over the phone. "That's all right," she said, not wanting to pressure him. "You tell me when it can be brought in for you to look at and we'll get along okay because we have another car." The man set a time, but instead of ending the conversation, he proceeded to talk with her at some length.

The car was towed in after 1 p.m. Her husband called in around 4 p.m. to see if they'd had a chance to find out what was wrong, only to be told that the car had been fixed—with a new starter already installed. When my friend dropped her husband off to get their car, the man remarked to him, "You have a pretty wife, don't you?" He was startled and asked if the man had met his wife to which the repairman replied, "No, but she's real nice to talk to." What a wonderful new definition of prettiness!

There was no need to pressure that man and he probably would not have performed well if he had been. My friend pushed *with* him instead of *against* him and likewise he pushed with her in having the car ready. Good lesson, don't you think! Being about our Father's business takes away the pressure of who wants what when. The Father's business is based on love and is the art of lovingly serving each other as we make our journey.

During a television interview, a sports figure was asked a number of questions pertaining to his abilities. Then came the request, "Now, tell us about the spiritual side of your life." I'm quite convinced that, in time to come, people will routinely inquire about another's spiritual journey. They will share their own progress while pointing out the ditches and detours they have encountered. Yes, our spiritual journey home will be common knowledge and a common goal. And our smaller outings and events along the way will carry vital information for other travelers.

A picture-perfect event!

Have you ever watched someone describe an outing or a vacation and seen them fairly glow at the thought of how picture perfect it was? It almost seems to be a badge of honor if nothing untoward occurred, as though our thinking had produced all this harmony and bliss. While our thinking may have a lot to do with what we attract to us, the appearance of weeds in our garden—the hitches in our perfect day—may not be anything we have invited. More than that, "the little hitch" may just be a perfect opportunity to do a small deed of kindness for someone else.

Two dear friends of mine accompanied me to New York in the winter of 1995 as I was giving talks in that city. The event's arranger saw to every little detail. She even had a couple of her friends put all three of us up at their homes. The talks went well and we had lovely visits. We even saw a Broadway musical.

My friends and I were further delighted when our kind hostesses took us to a quaint restaurant made from an old mill. Ah, another picture-perfect event was taking place. Well, not quite! Our waitress, who had a pronounced French accent, seemed uncooperative to say the least. It appeared she had no pleasure in waiting on us and hardly described the menu. We looked at each other and raised our eyebrows, but no one said a word. My friends were too kind to comment. As I puzzled over the situation, it seemed that something should be done, but what? I prayed about it, asking God how I could help. The thought quickly came to me, "Speak to her in French!"

Now, immediately I resisted this idea. My French was rusty so she might not understand me, and I could end up looking very silly indeed. On the other hand, what if she did understand me and wanted to carry on a conversation in French. Horrors, that was even worse! But did I really have a choice? So, when the waitress came close enough to me, I simply asked, "D'ou venez vous?" (Where do you come from?) She named a region in France, and when I said, "Oh?" she repeated it. I smiled, she smiled, and that was the end of the French conversation. It was also the end of the surly waitress. We now had a completely different woman serving us. She was full of smiles, made suggestions for our dessert, and even helped us on with our coats when we left.

On thinking about this later, I realized linguistic ability is totally inconsequential when one speaks in the language of love. Then I came across this statement made by Mary Baker Eddy under the title of "Heart to Heart." She wrote, "When the heart speaks, however simple the words, its language is always acceptable to those who have hearts." (*Miscellaneous Writings*, p. 262) What a truly loving heart our waitress must have had that only a few kind words would bring forth such a response.

Human reasoning isn't enough to tell us what another needs or why, but divine Love does know. If we ask the quiet question, in love, we'll receive Love's answer to the situation. So, was that trip "picture perfect"?   Absolutely, yes!   In fact, the mental picture I've retained of that lunch and the waitress was one of the highlights of the trip.

She's got the whole world in Her hands!

On frequent trips to a local place of business, I became acquainted with a young woman who was working very hard to better herself. Let's call this young woman "Sara." Despite her sad story, Sara was always "upbeat," a happy individual, and, a diligent worker with a very good heart.

Sara had numerous family difficulties with which to contend—helping to raise her drug-addicted sister's two boys and be a support to her dad who had physical problems. She also had a child of her own and had been on drugs herself at one point in her young life. And she was still only in her twenties when I met her. Sara told me that she was a smoker and had been for years, but very much wanted to overcome the addiction. Her dad was also a smoker and believed it wouldn't be possible for her to quit. Sara was praying about the situation and I offered to pray for her, too.   But the prayers seemed to no avail and the smoking continued.

Over the course of a few months, it became apparent that Sara didn't have a large wardrobe of clothes and depended mainly on a few outfits to wear to work. One day I suggested that we meet at a local store after her work hours so that I could buy her an outfit. Sara said I didn't need to do that, but eventually gratefully accepted. We met, shopped and giggled like two school girls as Sara tried on different clothes. There was a blue outfit that looked especially good on her, so I bought that and a blouse, and I believe Sara bought herself a blouse.

After this we treated ourselves to a sandwich together while Sara told me more details of her life. Her mother had passed on when she was sixteen and she had become pregnant at eighteen. Of course we talked about the smoking. Again, I assured her that it was not God's will for her that she be chained to a cigarette. She had her freedom and just needed to accept it. The truth was that her real nature was in the image and likeness of God and smoking just wasn't part of that spiritual nature. Sara nodded and we went on to other subjects. (By the way, I had not explained nor offered Christian Science treatment. I was simply praying for her.)

The very next day after our shopping trip, all desire for smoking left Sara. She couldn't stand the slightest smell of cigarettes. She washed her clothes, her hair and all her personal belongings. She even turned her purses inside out and scrubbed them thoroughly in order to rid them of every trace of the now-repugnant odor.

About a week later, Sara called me from work, knowing I'd be coming in during the day, and asked if I could bring her a blouse to wear because the one she had on still smelled of smoke. So, I went back to the store, found two on sale and took them to her. She bought one and I returned the other. Sara's release from the cigarette prison was complete, despite her dad's predictions and the fact that he still smoked at home. Her friends told her it was a miracle and couldn't believe it because they knew Sara had tried various remedies.

What happened? Why hadn't her prayers or my prayers been answered before the shopping trip? I think it was because they weren't backed up with something that was really needed in Sara's life. She needed to feel the mother-love of God. I believe it was the demonstration of that kind of love which helped free Sara.

That God is Mother as well as Father is becoming more universally accepted. For instance, at a recent outdoor interfaith event the audience was given handouts to sing "He's got the whole world in his hands." The second verse, as the speaker said, would give equal time to the motherhood of God so we sang, "She's got the little, tiny baby in Her hands. She's got the little, tiny baby in Her hands. She's got the little, tiny baby in Her hands. She's got the whole world in Her hands."

That shopping trip for Sara was totally in line with something James had touched on in his General Epistle. I quoted James at the beginning of this book as he talked about gifts and a perfect God who is unvarying. But, James wasn't merely urging us to receive these wonderful gifts of God. He obviously expected us to be ready to give them.

It was in the very next chapter that he made pointed remarks about partiality. He evidently didn't care for the custom (of his time and ours) of favoring the very important people—the VIPs—over others who are not so important . . . and for whom, of course, there is no acronym, as they are not important enough to warrant it. We all know about the CEO, but we don't talk about the MIC, the "mechanic in charge" at the gas station, do we? James goes on to rebuke those who simply talk a good game, but who don't "walk the talk." They may be spectators or critics, but they are not players on life's field.

These statements in James (2:15-16) pertained to Sara's situation. "If a brother or sister be naked, and destitute of daily food, And one of you say unto them, Depart in peace, be ye warmed and filled; notwithstanding ye give them not those things which are needful to the body; what doth it profit?" Well, Sara was a good distance from being naked but she surely had needs. Prayer alone, without filling that need, was not effective. It was necessary to show love in a tangible, motherly manner to this young woman. (Although I don't see or talk with Sara often, she has since sent me a Mother's Day card and has said on a few occasions that I was like a mother to her.)

James goes on after the quotation just mentioned to say that faith without works is dead. It's a wonderful discussion and James is very good company. (He's worth sitting down and having a cup of tea with anytime.) He's the one who talks about the tongue running away with us and then has a few blasting words for the rich engrossed in their riches. He does end, however, on the comforting note that the prayer of faith shall save the sick and sinners shall be forgiven.

Sara's life is continuing to flourish with more control over every aspect of it, not just cigarettes. She has become reunited with the father of her child and they are planning to be married. Her other relatives are being cared for elsewhere and Sara's work has provided her with advancements. She, like so many others, believes and trusts in the power of God. Sara loves good. (It is interesting that good was the term for God in the Anglo-Saxon and many other languages. People simply worshipped good.)

Not too long after the purchase for Sara, a friend of mine sent me a check and urged me to buy something for myself (she knew I was giving priority to my publishing activities). It was within a dollar or two of the amount I'd spent on Sara.

Answering the call.

Speaking of worshipping good, I'd like to relate what happened to a man who was sitting in a church service. My dad and I were visiting this man, who held a high church position, and he told us of the following incident. He attended church services in the headquarters of the church and was sitting in this large auditorium enjoying the service when suddenly the thought came to him to leave.

You can imagine this man's reaction to the idea of walking out of the church, and for no apparent reason. Here again, it is so necessary to listen to angel messages which, like the message to lean down to see the gas gauge, may not be irrelevant at all. Like that young man driving the van, our friend immediately dismissed the idea. In fact, he felt it was a suggestion to distract him.

However, when the idea came again and more strongly, he got up and walked out in the middle of the service. He said that people probably surmised he was in the grip of some kind of physical problem, but he couldn't be concerned about what others were thinking in the course of being obedient.

As he reached the street level, he saw a man sitting in a car staring at the church edifice. Our friend approached and asked the man if he could be of any assistance. The stranger then admitted, "I've always wondered what this church was all about, but never had the courage to go in." It was good our friend had the courage to go out! He offered to explain the basic concepts of the religion to the stranger, who immediately accepted the invitation.

So, for the remainder of the church service our friend sat in the car with that man, performing another service. He shared what he knew of God's goodness. The stranger's quiet question had been heard, and divine Love had sent our friend out with the answer.

Serving through prayer.

The world, our government, our community, individuals constantly seek better answers. Like the church member who met the man in the car, we can be part of how divine Love meets human needs. The wonderful thing about prayer is its applicability to every nation or situation. True, selfless prayer is not confined to any one denomination or governmental body. Prayer is not only nonpolitical, it is apolitical. At the point one prays for a just government they have, in effect, jumped off any political bandwagon. It's a wise move because no one party is all right or all wrong all the time.

We can hope and pray for the most honest, sincere and wise candidate to be elected, but the human view of government or of justice is always flawed. The divine view—how God sees the government of His own universe—is truly the only right view and prayer enables us to see a little more clearly what God sees and knows. While human judgments as to the best way to defend our freedoms may vary widely, there is one solution that never varies and never errs and that is the divine solution.

If we really desire to see peace, some radical thinking will be necessary. Paul's peace plan was to pray for all those in authority (I Timothy 2:1,2) and not to be immersed in the human condition—"the things of the flesh" but to pursue "the things of the Spirit," (Romans 8: 5,6). He ended this latter counsel with the rather startling statement: "For to be carnally minded is death; but to be spiritually minded is life and peace."

Terrorist acts at home or abroad will be neutralized by prayer that is based on God's allness and goodness, prayer that is motivated by impartial love, prayer that penetrates any hidden system of wickedness. Whether it's a city gang or an international terrorist cell, these are all a type of business—but certainly not the Father's business, no matter what name they may parade under or assume.

These illegal businesses are based on fear, hate, competition, feelings of unworthiness, religious fanaticism, selfishness and any other such untoward emotions. To concentrate on the salesmen attached to the business—the gang members or the terrorists involved—doesn't really provide a permanent solution because new salesmen can always be recruited. The business will pick up the unemployed and unemployable segments of society who are open or addicted to the above emotions.

A few years ago, there was a type of vandalism being enacted periodically in certain public sectors of my community and it was quite dangerous. It became apparent I needed to serve the community through prayer. First of all, I recognized that God's kingdom was indeed under perfect control and that what appeared to be human hate was illegitimate and didn't belong in His kingdom. His children are all peace-loving and gentle spiritual beings who are in the Father's business, the business of love. The human view of lawlessness was a lie about God's children.

On that solid basis of spiritual conviction, I then prayed for that hateful type of thinking to be removed from human consciousness. " Dear Father-Mother, may no one know or be conscious of committing harm in this manner. May hate, fear and violence be removed from the community's consciousness and be seen as the nothingness they truly are. May there be no individual to represent this type of lawlessness and may each individual be attracted to only what is good and loving. May this sinful purpose be wiped out and there be no adherents of it. Thank you Father-Mother, God." Immediately, the activity ceased. A few days later, one more incident was reported. I prayed again. That was the last time I heard of it. Whether it was the prayer of one or of many, I am convinced that prayer took care of that situation.

It's a little like praying that a certain business be denied a business license and that there should be no sales staff for that business. When you go to the underlying problem and neutralize it, then the business is out of business. Vandalism or terrorism is an illegal business. God does not license it and because it is unlawful in a divine sense we can outlaw it, too—not only by better human laws but by the law of prayer. Prayer doesn't need to wait for committee action or votes. Prayer penetrates to every cell of terrorism and goes to the heart of the matter. It virtually says to the wicked motives and activity (not the salesmen), "You are a liar and an impostor. You lie as to man's true nature and you think to pose a threat to the everpresence of divine Love. I pray that you—hate or malice—be banished from this unlawful business of vandalism and I pray that you can mislead no one into representing your wrong intentions."

That's what happened to the car mechanic who wanted to punch Glen. Through his unselfish and heartfelt prayers, Glen actually canceled out the business of hate, retaliation or even impatience. These were not viable states of thinking and had no business being in business. The Father's business is always based on goodwill and love. By realizing the impossibility of the wrong business, Glen took himself out of it, replacing his impatience with love. The car mechanic was suddenly taken out of the retaliation business and seemed to lose all memory of it. The wrong business was denied a license and the salesmen were released, discharged. Glen and the mechanic were both free to go on with a better sense of business—the business of serving each other with lovingkindness.

Interestingly, sometimes all that is needed is for citizens to make the decision to take back their community from the drug dealers or other harmful and disruptive elements. The firm decision to outlaw the illegal activity can result in banishing it without a gunshot or a fight. The community stands united on the mental conviction that the activity cannot be tolerated because it is out of line with goodness. Evil is an outlaw and is outlawed. It truly is a mental decision.

The temptation is to make a human being or a nation our enemy. Goliath said, ". . .give me a man that we may fight together" (I Samuel 17:10). And what happened? A lowly shepherd boy with a slingshot, five smooth stones and no armor (no human weaponry) came up to meet him and defeated him. I like to think of the five stones that David used as spiritual senses that take over and aim at the so-called intelligence or power of matter and defeat it.

Paul who had done his fair (or rather unfair) share of warring against people finally had a whole different "take" or perspective on getting rid of what is troublesome. He told the Ephesians to be strong in God and in His power. "For we wrestle not against flesh and blood, but against principalities, against powers, against the rulers of the darkness of this world, against spiritual wickedness in high places" (Ephesians 6:12). Then he went on to describe the armor and weapons needed for this invisible combat: truth, righteousness, the gospel of peace, faith, salvation and the sword of the Spirit, which he defined as the Word of God.

It's taking warfare to a whole new level to deal with the invisible darkness called hatred, fear or oppression. But that's the level at which Jesus fought the battle and won. His lines of communication to headquarters, to his Father, never could be broken or jammed by enemy fire. He never let his spiritual guard down. While nations take steps to handle conflict and terrorism (and while we pray for our government and military men and women), it is also wise to consider how we may individually and collectively follow Jesus in his victory over human wrath or hatred.

When my dad was held in solitary confinement for three months as a prisoner of war during World War II he received an angel message to control his thinking. He wrote: "From that moment, fearful suggestions, resentful suggestions, hateful suggestions were barred from entering my consciousness." He went on to say, ". . . through my newfound thinking a more spiritual sense of life was beginning to dawn on me. I saw the battle was no longer with people and circumstances but with false thinking, which was constantly being corrected and defeated by true thinking" (*The Ultimate Freedom*, p. 17). He literally followed Christ Jesus by taking the battle to higher ground.

Dealing with false thinking is the solution whether we are individually or collectively at risk. However, it's the level we are least likely to choose as a battleground. This takes effort and self-control, but it brings great rewards. The church with the large outdoor sign posted this saying: "If you have no enemy within then the enemy without cannot harm you."

It has been said that this earthly life is a school filled with a multitude of lessons. Now, if there were a harmful subject being taught at a public university—perhaps a class in hatred and the weaponry involved—then a petition might be signed by many students to ask for the removal of the subject from the school's curriculum.

Our collective prayers are like that petition being circulated on the grounds that the subject of terrorism should not be allowed in our earthly school system because it does not appear in heaven's list of subjects. We petition the head of life's school, our Principle of life, that this harmful subject be removed so that no one may take the class. It may be necessary to reestablish our spiritual basis by attaining a clearer consciousness of reality first, by denying the wrong as being part of God's universe and protesting or affirming the truth of being, for it is on this basis that our petition will be circulated. In a way, this basis is a preamble to the petition.

As *Science and Health* states the spiritual fact: "The universe of Spirit is peopled with spiritual beings, and its government is divine Science" (p. 264). Then we can pray fervently, unselfishly, for that divine fact to be made humanly apparent.

The same method may be employed to eradicate disease that is trying to make the rounds in the community or in the world. With the clear recognition that no microbe of misery lurks in the atmosphere of God, we are equipped to do victorious battle against such insinuations regarding our sphere of being. God's heavenly atmosphere of thought is an arena of the divine Mind and is always pure and healthgiving. Because the disease does not exist in God's atmosphere, it can be outlawed from our human experience. It cannot insinuate itself, or "worm its way," into our lives. Again, we may circulate our petition on these grounds and have the disease removed as a subject from earth's school. Once removed as a subject, it cannot manifest itself as an object. It cannot be objectified on the human body.

Any untoward circumstance that arises is not the human interrupting divine harmony. The human cannot intervene into the divine (and the situation does not require the divine to intervene in the human). Rather, it is the opportunity for the human mind to yield to, agree with, the divine Mind.

We need to arrive at the place where the prayer and the answer meet, where the human coincides with the divine. In his book, Revelation, John the beloved disciple of Jesus looked deeply into spiritual history, past and future, and saw Jesus' place in it. Commenting on this, Mary Baker Eddy wrote, "John saw the human and divine coincidence, shown in the man Jesus, as divinity embracing humanity in Life and its demonstration,—reducing to human perception and understanding the Life which is God" (*Science and Health*, p. 561).

Jesus' whole life was a prayer of this coincidence of the human with the divine. This is the power point of the human experience and there is none other for the human does not contain any power of its own, though it may reflect the divine power. To bring the human picture into focus with harmony and brotherly love, the human must coincide or agree with the divine.

If we will form that human coalition of brotherhood which, full of love for all mankind, prays for its enemies as well as friends; if we will pray to our divine authority to remove that subject of terrorism and to eliminate any cell of hatred; if we will break away from political scrimmage lines to cast our vote for the divine goal, we will find the wrong subject will wane in human consciousness. It will be removed from our earthly school's catalogue of classes. Hatred will become out of date, out of vogue, out of thought.

If we pray not only for that subject to be removed but also pray that no individual be misled to sign up for and enter that classroom of hate, then our prayer will deter the footsteps of the unwary. Our prayer must be so lacking human leanings, politics, and opinions and so full of love for our neighbor that God will recognize this desire—love for one's neighbor—as His own divine idea for the government of His universe. As this prayer is recognized by God, it is answered and the human circumstance that accompanies the prayer will yield to the divine. That yielding is the healing.

Prayer does make a difference. It's the best peace pact ever formed. There are peace demonstrations which are truly peaceful and there are those that demonstrate anything but peace. So, how can we sell the world on peace? What sales approach can we use?

May we have a demonstration, please?

There are numerous approaches to selling. A salesman might continually call a prospect until the prospect is convinced and becomes a customer. Or there is the demonstration route—show how the product works and it will sell itself. The first approach usually entails much tenacity and either one's own belief in the product or simply the desire to make a sale. However, nothing can quite replace the authenticity of a demonstration. Show the customer what the product does and let the customer decide. In the sales arena these are the "features"—what it does—and "benefits"—how it impacts the customer.

Christianity was promoted and accepted by demonstration. It was demonstrated by healing the sick, reforming the sinner, and raising the dead or dying. The disciples went from town to town with the purpose of demonstrating how good God is. Jesus was the highest demonstrator of divine power the world has ever known. He even allowed himself to be used as part of the demonstration when he underwent the crucifixion and proved that Christianity and his understanding of God, who is Life, would not fail him.

Science and Health speaks about this (p. 42): "The resurrection of the great demonstrator of God's power was the proof of his final triumph over body and matter, and gave full evidence of divine Science,— evidence so important to mortals. The belief that man has existence or mind separate from God is a dying error. This error Jesus met with divine Science and proved its nothingness."

If all who are so intent upon persuading others to believe in God would replace this with the demonstration of God's power and goodness, that would be a sales competition worth entering. Who can show the most love? Who can most effectively sell this concept by being an example of it to others? If we'd like to sell others on goodness, let us be good. If we'd like to sell the world on peace, let us show peace in our family and business contacts. If we'd like to convince others of God's power, let us show them by healing the sick, reforming the sinner, and raising the dying (yes, even the dead). The war of words, or of religious swords, cannot replace the peace of performance. And we can always begin with small deeds—no need to walk on water as the first demonstration to others of the power of Spirit over matter.

Mary Baker Eddy, who had proved the power and value of the Science of Christianity for nine years before undertaking to publish her main work on the subject (a refreshing approach, don't you agree!), wrote in *Science and Health* (p. 329): "A little understanding of Christian Science proves the truth of all that I say of it. Because you cannot walk on the water and raise the dead, you have no right to question the great might of divine Science in these directions. Be thankful that Jesus, who was the true demonstrator of Science, did these things, and left his example for us. In Science we can use only what we understand. We must prove our faith by demonstration."

A little girl, who brought in a free soap-powder sample from the mailbox, thoughtfully said to her mother, "Jesus was like a free sample of God." Yes, we can each be a free sample of goodness to our community and our world.

The demonstration of God's goodness is the best church service we can provide. As *Science and Health* clearly states on page 40, "It is sad that the phrase *divine service* has come so generally to mean public worship instead of daily deeds." As we rethink our "divine service," gone will be the accusation, "We're holding a church service and you better be there!" to be replaced with the gentility of, "I'm performing this service (this good deed, anywhere, anytime) because you *are* here!" That's what the Good

Samaritan did when he came to the wounded man's aid. That's what the man did who walked out of the church service to be of service to the man in the car. Yes, serving does the win the game, and it is indeed a love match!

A change in the mental climate.

Times and needs are changing and the challenge is to stay abreast of them. It would often appear as though we make our customs inflexible while allowing the Word of God to be flexible. It should be the other way around. Our divine Principle is changeless and unchangeable, but our customs and opinions should be easily changed to adapt to current needs.

A mental climate change can be as obvious as the change of climate on the Big Island of Hawaii. When Glen and I lived there we were told by locals that the weather made a noticeable transition at a certain intersection in Waimea (also called Kamuela). And it was true. You could feel the colder, damper atmosphere on one corner and the drier, warmer air on the other. It was quite remarkable.

During that period, in 1992, we noticed a shift taking place in the mental climate. These winds of change were even stronger than the trade winds of the Islands. We met two women who had formerly belonged to a religious community on the Mainland. They were now carrying on a secular life, which they described as spiritual rather than religious. Our interest was piqued so we engaged in conversations with them about spirituality.

This prompted a visit to the large bookstore in Kona, where we asked how many of their books fell into the self-help or spirituality category. They said 40 percent of their books were on that subject. Here was an obvious clue! People were actually looking in bookstores for spiritual help. For many centuries that had been the territory of the church alone. So, it appeared that another type of sales force was invading the church's territory, and with a different approach. Just how different was it?

The distinction sometimes made as to spirituality being a lone course and religion being a collective activity is not totally accurate. Both include solitary and congregational endeavors. People interested in spirituality regularly congregate in brotherly fashion in seminars and in chat rooms on the Internet. Those termed religious often study quietly at home during the week. The difference is organization. But organizations vary in their ability to enact true church. Sometimes there's very little brotherhood or usefulness evident in an organization, while brotherhood may be practiced by a single stranger on the street!

Today, articles attest to the fact that the face of church in general is changing. Some congregations are adopting the "go-and-tell" instead of the "come-and-hear" policy. And many mainline denominations in the United States and other countries are experiencing a decline in attendance while nondenominational churches may be booming.

While eating lunch at an outdoor café, a stranger and I had a discussion on this very subject. She said that even as a child she couldn't understand why—on the main intersection of her little town in the Midwest—there was a different Christian church on each of the four corners. To her youthful eyes this was very puzzling indeed. Weren't they all Christian? she wondered. (She now belongs to a large nondenominational Christian Church, that holds many services on Sundays to accommodate their more than three thousand members.)

Just as small, individually-owned bookstores are being replaced by the mega-bookstores (wasn't the film "You've Got Mail!" not only a sweet story but a poignant example of a vanishing era?), some smaller churches are being replaced with the mega-church. But this is the quantum era (filled with quantities of collectives rather than individualism) and we can expect to see changes again. Like a reviving fashion, styles may return but never quite in the same form. However, the mega-church is surely evidence of dissolving doctrinal barriers, which (like the fall of the Berlin Wall) could signal greater freedom for mankind.

How does a changing church fit in with the emergence of the spiritual group? It appears we have a newer and friendlier version of the old range wars that took place in pioneer days between the cattlemen and the sheep farmers. Today, the spirituality turf is being disputed by the religious and the spiritual. It is argued by the religious that they have a more structured and protected brotherhood than the spiritual ones who journey too freely and independently. Meanwhile, the spiritual group claim they are unhampered, free to roam the spiritual range. They even suggest that the religious are fenced in by form. It's an ongoing discussion that we might possibly (perhaps a little irreverently) put under two headings: "You need to be corralled. Shape up and sing right!" and "I like to sing on the open range. Don't fence me in."

Perhaps this would be a good time to remember the little saying (from where I don't know): "All God's children sing in the choir—some sing lower, some sing higher, some sing high as the telephone wire." It sounds a trifle nonsensical but it carries a spiritually sound message: There are countless ways of singing God's praises.

Yes, the manner in which one should worship is no longer set in ecclesiastical concrete. Just as many choose a sit-down meal in a restaurant, there are those who enjoy listening to a sermon sitting in a church edifice. Others might prefer a television sermon as their take-out food. The Internet, seminars, and books feed seekers and browsers, while the home-schooled in spirituality can also make good progress. During the religious era, God-fearing men and women all attended church services. But in today's scientific era such attendance is no longer the standard of devotion. In changing times, it's difficult to judge just how another should demonstrate their love for God and man, isn't it! As long as the two great loves are in place the journey can continue. They keep us on target and provide us with traveling companions.

The unity question.

Anyone who has ever worked with a group of people knows that the greatest challenge is usually that of differing opinions. "I did it my way" may be a pretty song, but it's not a pretty picture. A steamroller approach doesn't produce harmony, speed the journey, or make for success. More than that, it's a detour. Yes, pushing through, and getting one's own way, is a pretty good indication that we are off our spiritual path.

It takes humble listening to the divine Mind to gain a better sense of direction. The mental compass also needs to point north, to our Principle, constantly and automatically. With everyone taking that true bearing, unity of mind becomes possible.

We think of unity as working harmoniously together and, of course, that is true. We can all express unity but (and this is an important point) we don't create unity by expressing it. Unity—like mercy, love, or goodness—is a concept that already exists. It is there to be demonstrated, just as math functions are available to be put into practice. Goodness (and everything included in that broad concept) forms its own unity. This divine unity of good may be reflected in an individual's adherence to goodness and by brotherhood. The higher unity is man's unity with his Maker. That comes first. The second unity is the brotherhood seen in action.

This was brought home vividly to me one day at the recording studio. The project was "Lessons from Bird," in which are described some of the spiritual lessons learned on Palomar Mountain. One of the four songs to be included was of the city described in Revelation as being foursquare. The lyrics were based on the explanation in *Science and Health* (pages 575-577) and the music was Brahms' Lullaby. Three of my young friends from the children's song and dance studio were to sing it for me. They already knew the Brahms melody and the words seemed simple enough, so I didn't give them a full preparation for this event.

First of all, we recorded each child separately—singing the whole song—to have some solo parts available. Then they sang it together (well, not really together as it turned out). After the children left, it became obvious that they were slightly out of time with each other now and then. This posed quite a problem. No matter how we juggled the different tracks by bringing in solo parts here and there, the result was the same. And though we had a couple of group tracks, we just couldn't get it quite right.

As a last-ditch effort, I asked that all their solo tracks be put together instead of trying to work with the ones they had sung in unison. The sound engineer was appalled at the idea and told me we couldn't do that. Oh, he didn't mean we couldn't do it technically because he could do just about anything. When a singer on a previous CD hadn't finished the "d" on "bend," my expert copied and pasted this sound from another word, and the result was seamless.

However, he really balked at this new request. Musically, it was not possible to put together three separate solo tracks and have them work as unison singing. It simply couldn't happen. As I prayed about it, the answer still came to do just that. So I finally said, "Please humor me, and put them together." With doubt and reluctance, he complied.

As the singing progressed from line to line and verse to verse, the engineer's comments went from, "Amazing!" to "Incredible!" to "Impossible!" The children were actually singing their solo parts together! What had happened? The idea contained in the song was greater than the effort to sing in unison, is the only explanation. Each child had individually sung the idea. In turn that idea had brought them together.

What a wonderful lesson for members of any group formed for a good purpose! Stay focused on the idea that brought the members together in the first place and never lose sight of it. If each individual understandingly does his or her part—with that good goal in mind—then unity, harmony and oneness of mind will be seen in the group's activity.

The challenge of serving together.

Many years ago, I read a book which related "successful" and "unsuccessful" endeavors. Included was the story of a popular Boston restaurant. This restaurant was begun with the idea of providing very fine service. In fact, it served the customers so well that business boomed and a second restaurant was opened. Then something happened: The business declined and eventually the restaurant failed. Imbued with its success, the restaurant had focused on its own needs rather than serving the customers. It turned inward.

This temptation to turn inward is the challenge any worthwhile organization will doubtless face. If the temptation is accepted then the organization begins to serve its own ends, forgetting the purpose for which it was founded. It loses the vision of the founder, exchanging it for the interests of the organization. The members may wonder what is going on with management.

The same may be true of individual members of an organization. For example, church members, who follow the teachings of an able pastor, might begin with the honest and high intention of serving others. Then as the challenge appears, the individuals succumb to the alluring arguments of self-serving and use the precious knowledge for their own comfort and success. The pastor may wonder what is going on with the members.

But even those members who work diligently and unselfishly in a worthwhile organization may, on occasion, feel trapped by their service. As Christ Jesus came to show us spiritual freedom, no loving individual (following his lead) would accept a trap for themselves or impose it on others. And a collective trap is no holier than an individual one. Serving, as Jesus practiced it, was an unselfish freeing activity, not bound servitude.

An article, originally published in England during the early 1900s under the title of "Servants of the Spirit," warns of the pitfalls of organization, citing both government and organized religion as examples. The political or religious leanings of the author, W. J. Brown, are not defined as he comes to a simple but profound conclusion. The article begins: "There are many classifications into which men and women may be divided—as upper, middle, or lower class; rich, well-to-do, and poor; religious, sceptical, and atheist; Conservative, Liberal, Labour; Catholic, Protestant; master and man; and so forth and so on, *ad infinitum*. But, as I think, the only categorization which really matters is that which divides men as between the Servants of the Spirit and the Prisoners of the Organization. That classification, which cuts right across all the other classifications, is indeed the fundamental one."

Brown's "straight-from-the-shoulder," well-reasoned article discusses what occurs after an organization is formed around an idea: "It is that, the idea having given birth to the organization, the organization develops a self-interest, which has no connection with, and becomes inimical to, the idea with which it began. Now the thing which permits this process of diversion to take place, so that the organization comes to stand for the opposite of the idea which originally inspired it, is the tendency in men and women to become Prisoners of the Organization, instead of being Servants of the Spirit."

Many excellent thinkers have pondered deeply the issues of organization. Glen and I met such an individual on Palomar Mountain. We sat by the glowing fireplace in his small cabin as this man described his findings on the subject. I'm not sure if he had written a book, but he did give talks on the nine stages that organizations pass through from their inception to their end. He discussed points of entrepreneurship and early and later bureaucracy. It was a sobering conversation, but it did propel us into more spiritual views of God's ways and means.

Concerns over human organization are not without foundation. For many years now, the public has been informed of frayed business ethics as well as questionable accounting practices. In 2003, television news even showed a CEO being taken from his building in handcuffs. The disbursement of relief funds and the profits of philanthropic organizations have likewise come under close scrutiny. The full report on that is yet to come.

Organized religion has fared no better. For decades, reports of moral lapses and crimes of money mismanagement have been rather frequent and not confined to any one denomination. Difficulties evidently arise due to a departure from the principles on which the organization was founded and possibly from a misunderstanding of the rules of that organization. Yes, how to accomplish worthwhile endeavors through organization without incurring its abuses is a knotty problem.

There exists another important consideration for any spiritual thinker. Material organization should not assume a position of power in one's own thinking, as power is not material but spiritual. Personal adulation and unqualified trust in material organization have led many a group, large and small, to follow a charismatic leader into the abyss of infamy.

Organization seeks to build itself up and trusts in numbers to enable it to act powerfully. (Let's lose weight individually, but gain weight collectively to be really effective.) Large numbers do not empower, but large ideas do. A single individual, such as Jesus, has changed the course of human history, not to mention the calendar in the greater part of the world.

Interestingly, Gideon, who was to go up against the Midianites, received the heavenly command to *reduce* his forces.

"And the Lord said unto Gideon, The people that are with thee are too many for me to give the Midianites into their hands, lest Israel vaunt themselves against me, saying, Mine own hand hath saved me" (Judges 7:2). They were not to be permitted to trust in numbers but in the power of God.

The whittling-down process began by requesting that those who were afraid should turn back. Twenty-two thousand returned and ten thousand remained. This was still too many so the host of men were put to a test at the water's edge. Three hundred men—who lapped water by putting their hands to their mouths—were chosen. The others—who bowed down to drink—were released and sent back home. This seems to imply that watchfulness is requisite. Obviously, those that bowed down couldn't see what was happening around them. The three hundred chosen men were triumphant after one of the most unusual "military" encounters one could imagine, as told throughout the seventh chapter of Judges. Courage, watchfulness and obedience won the day. Difficult to purchase those qualities in a military-supply store!

"The central fact of the Bible is the superiority of spiritual over physical power" (*Science and Health*, p. 131). If we are to agree with this, then plainly the world is in need of a change of values, of thought currency. (This may take far more effort than changing over to the Euro but will bring much greater rewards of unity.) Yes, a thought conversion is necessary—not to convert others to religious creeds or beliefs but to convert thinking from reliance on material means to a reliance on spiritual means. In this thought conversion, the divine Mind, God, would have the first and final say. And it would surely be possible for a small number, truly united under this one Mind, to effect that changeover.

It was apparently this type of conversion to which Mary Baker Eddy referred when telling a class of only 65 people that, "We, to-day, in this class-room, are enough to convert the world if we are of one Mind; for then the whole world will feel the influence of this Mind; as when the earth was without form, and Mind spake and form appeared" (*Miscellaneous Writings*, p. 279).

And Christ Jesus had said, ". . . if two of you shall agree on earth as touching any thing that they shall ask, it shall be done for them of my Father which is in heaven. For where two or three are gathered together in my name, there am I in the midst of them" (Matthew 18:19,20). Christ Jesus did not advocate a powerful human organization with which to accomplish spiritual goals.

That Mary Baker Eddy thought and prayed deeply about this subject is apparent from her statements on organization. It was necessary to think in this direction as her discovery had not found a ready home in other churches, though it rescued many a parishioner from the grave. So how best to share this healing discovery with the world? was the question. She had written that, "The vital part, the heart and soul of Christian Science, is Love" (*Science and Health*, p. 113). How can one organize Love which is God, or even the love that is expressed by humanity?

Her reluctance to form an organization is evident from an early statement: "It is not indispensable to organize materially Christ's church. It is not absolutely necessary to ordain pastors and to dedicate churches; but if this be done, let it be in concession to the period, and not as a perpetual or indispensable ceremonial of the church." As she continues to explain this "concession to the period," it becomes obvious that she is making a distinction between church and organization: "If our church is organized, it is to meet the demand, 'Suffer it to be so now.' The real Christian compact is love for one another" (*Miscellaneous Writings*, p. 91).

In making a concession to the needs of the times, Mrs. Eddy followed Jesus' example as he allowed John to baptize him on the basis of ". . . Suffer it to be so now: for thus it becometh us to fulfil all righteousness . . . " (Matthew 3:15).

Her ensuing organization went through many stages, as did the very well attended Massachusetts Metaphysical College she founded. Such popularity would have pleased most founders, but not Mary Baker Eddy—due to her spiritual foresight: "The apprehension of what has been, and must be, the final outcome of material organization, which wars with Love's spiritual compact, caused me to dread the unprecedented popularity of my College" (*Retrospection and Introspection*, p. 47).

After closing her College, she later reopened it, in a scaled-back form, as auxiliary to her church. Her resulting By-Laws for the Church were contained in an amazingly slim and streamlined *Church Manual*. There were no reams of regulations and rules to wade through. Known for her compassion and motherliness, the Discoverer of Christian Science devoted all her time and energy to the task at hand—that of helping to free humanity from the bondage of sin, disease and death. According to her own statements, organization was a means to an end, and it was even open-ended (though not often perceived that way). As a true "Servant of the Spirit," it would not be part of Mary Baker Eddy's purpose to allow organization to take prisoners.

Evidently, human nature shackles itself with organizational modes just as it binds itself with material laws of sickness and health. This fleshly nature might be thought of as the "opposition party" which is opposed to man's true freedom. Paul stated the "carnal mind is enmity against God" (Romans 8:7). *Science and Health* (p. 151) agrees, "The human mind is opposed to God and must be put off, as St. Paul declares." Human pride, fear, competition, desire for ease, trust in matter and other unseemly ingredients are all found within the human mind. The enmity, or opposition, of the carnal mind is evident in its unwillingness to transfer allegiance from matter to Spirit, all the while claiming its own brand of spirituality. That's why it is the "opposition party."

Now, it is helpful to look up definitions. The definition of divine is "relating to God." The definition of human is "relating to man." (And "man" may be an individual, specific term or it may be a collective or generic term that includes men, women and children.) As everything is, in truth, part of God's creation, all relates to Him, including man. All is, in actual fact, divine. So spiritual man is a divine idea of God, and relates, or belongs, to God. No qualities of being or abilities belong to man except what he receives from God and he has these only by reflection. The image and likeness of God, like an image in a mirror, can do nothing on its own but reflects the original. Jesus said this plainly, ". . . The Son can do nothing of himself, but what he seeth the Father do: for what things soever he doeth, these also doeth the Son likewise" (John 5:19).

The opposition to God appears as mortal man continually attempts to relate everything back to himself, either as an individual or as a collective. He claims a human identity instead of a divine one. He obeys his own human will instead of the divine will. He trusts human government more than the divine government. He desires a human kingdom instead of the kingdom of heaven.

Relating everything back to man, instead of to God, virtually makes the "effect" the "cause." This is an impossible human belief which shows itself as matter and all forms of limitation. It is mortal, so it dies. The human cannot attain divine status by claiming that what belongs to God actually belongs to man instead. Impossible desires, such as the appropriation of the divine by the human, are the clouds—"life's illusions"—that are being dispelled on our journey of discovering Truth. We arrive home only as the human errors evaporate and we face reality—"the new heaven and earth" that are not material, and do not belong to man, but to God.

This is what Jesus demonstrated. He proved that all belongs to God. We don't have a life separate from Life to live. We don't have a love separate from Love to enact. We don't have a truth separate from Truth to know. How reassuring this is, because man can't lose what God owns. He can't lose the life of Life, the truth of Truth, or the love of Love. The divine monopoly on creation does not limit man in God's image and likeness but, on the contrary, fully empowers him. In a Bible Lesson on spiritual sonship, Mary Baker Eddy stated, " Man is God's image and likeness; whatever is possible to God, is possible to man *as God's reflection*" (*Miscellaneous Writings*, p. 183).

One good method of reversing the erroneous human tendency described above, is to remember that we are on a spiritual journey. Obviously, we can't be heaven-bound and earth-bound at the same time. (And "bound" can be taken two ways—both as a direction and as a state of being.) If we bind ourselves to the true facts of spiritual being and determine to practice them we will secure our direction to heavenly harmony. We will not be bound, or captured, by the earth, moving in the direction of mortality.

Wisely, lovingly serving God and man inevitably frees us from self-imposed chains of false human duties and leads us to divinely-inspired activities. We will no longer be prisoners of human circumstances or of organizations but joyful servants of the Spirit. The way has been shown us.

Releasing the Way-shower.

Unfortunately, Christ Jesus has been appropriated by the religious community on behalf of theology and confined to, and filed under, the religious category. Individuals who are simply spiritual seekers, or those mainly interested in medicine and science, have no real knowledge that Jesus is actually showing everyone the way out of a limited material and mortal sense of life. Let's open that file folder and generously distribute this information to all who feel there has to be more to life than what we see here.

Jesus' demonstrations of spiritual power should be and are a tremendous help to the scientific community. Jesus had a science far beyond anything the world has known. He also had a medicine that has been unparalleled by medical science. The way home to spiritual reality has been well defined for us. If we would release the Way-shower and not insist that he belong only to the religious, we may be surprised to find that countless people truly worship good, and wish to walk in that pathway.

The way of the Christ, Truth, is narrow only in that it allows no deviation (no sideways journey off our spiritual base) but it is broad in its appeal and love. Yes, it is broad enough to include universal humanity.

The adversarial nature of human nature—warring against the spirituality of the Christ, Truth—would keep Jesus from being accepted as the Way-shower out of matter. This adversary, called by many names—be it devil, Belial, the accuser or the carnal mind—is merely the supposed opposite of Spirit claiming power in matter. Christ Jesus, in his mission, poked holes all through this supposed opposite by proving material laws to be counterfeit, bogus. Spiritual law supported all that he did. Spirituality was the truth of being he demonstrated, and spiritual power was all-powerful. Matter, with its material laws, was proved at every step to be a nonentity in the world of Spirit—our true home.

Despite human misunderstanding or misuse of the most precious message that mankind has ever received, the Christ, Truth, is still knocking at the door of human consciousness. The spiritual answer to the human, material plight of sin, disease and death is not going to disappear. Even if we misunderstand it, misuse it, try to toss it aside or misfile it, the answer will still be there. It is waiting to bless and lead us home.

A progressive worship.

The Bible actually provides us with a timeline—a record of man's progress on his spiritual journey home. The corporeal concept of God as a vengeful or manlike deity finally gives way to the incorporeal idea of God, who is divine Love. Today's progressive, spiritual thinker will not demand that God be a material being made in mortal man's image and likeness but will allow for the spiritual fact that man is, in reality, a spiritual being made in God's image and likeness. God and His spiritual idea, called man, never changed in all of human history, but mortal man's idea of God certainly did. This gradual transition can be seen throughout the Old to the New Testament.

The same progress is required in worship, which appears to go through three stages. First is the worship of a place. Earthly locations become designated as holy land and unholy wars are fought over them. Secondly, we may progress to a place of worship. Beautiful buildings arise which inspire and delight. Others are invited to join the brotherhood that holds worship services in that place. And in case one should become enamored of a building, Mary Baker Eddy defines its purpose: "Our proper reason for church edifices is, that in them Christians may worship God,— not that Christians may worship church edifices!" (*Miscellany*, p. 162).

Finally, progress is made to the invisible stage—making place for worship in one's daily life. Everywhere one goes is a holy place, everyone one meets is a brother or sister, and service is performed daily in deeds that bless. Yes, mankind will progress from worshipping a place to a place for worship, until we finally make place for worshipping daily in the spirit of truth and of love.

Originally "church" in the New Testament referred to a band of followers—believers in the power and goodness of God. It was not a building. That's how Paul could say in his Epistle to the Romans (16:3,5) "Greet Priscilla and Aquila my helpers in Christ Jesus: . . . Likewise greet the church that is in their house."

Church and building have become so synonymous that many fight to maintain a building when the effort should be made on the side of supporting the brotherhood and their enactment of church. How can this brotherhood better function today is a good question and requires us to "discern the signs of the times," as

Jesus urged (Matthew 16:3). Change is inevitable on the human scene. It's no good insisting on making buggy wheels for the automobile showroom down the road. They are not going to sell. Change is not fatal to progress, but losing the way would be!

When finding ourselves in changing terrain or unknown territory, we sometimes act as does a bird that has become trapped behind large glass windows. We flap our mental wings more vigorously and keep demanding of ourselves that we try harder. The real need, and simple answer, is to look for the open door. And there is always an open door, as was told to the church of Philadelphia (those followers filled with brotherly love): ". . . I have set before thee an open door, and no man can shut it; . . . ." (Revelation 3:8). We are never trapped!

Over the years, I've heard from people who were concerned about the changing appearance of church, so this poem was written in response to those calls for comfort.

As The Waters Cover The Sea.*

Our church is not where it appears to be,
That building down the block.
It isn't fortified by windows closed
Or door with heavy lock.

That building is just a vessel
To travel earth's rough sea;
It helps convey the message
Of God's love for you and me.

If changing times necessitate
That our vessel we reconsider,
Humbly we'll listen for Mind's design
For God is the only Giver.

He gives and fills our joyful days,
With grace He does us feed,
Not as we plan, for it is Love divine
That meets all human need.

So with grateful thanks we can accept
Any needful change,
For if a new vessel we have to choose,
It will doubtless have more range.

But if that vessel should falter,
And should it eventually fail,
Then we'll each be a little vessel
And set out under full sail.

We'll fly flags of truth, send signals of love,
A flotilla our church will be,
And God's glory will fill every part of the earth,
As the waters cover the sea.

*Habakkuk 2:14

The Samaritan woman, whom Jesus asked for a drink of water, perceived that he was a prophet. So she asked him about worship: "Our fathers worshipped in this mountain; and ye say, that in Jerusalem is the place where men ought to worship" (John 4:20). Jesus answered her, "Woman, believe me, the hour cometh, when ye shall neither in this mountain, nor yet at Jerusalem, worship the Father." And he continued, "But the hour cometh, and now is, when the true worshippers shall worship the Father in spirit and in truth: for the Father seeketh such to worship him. God is a Spirit: and they that worship him must worship him in spirit and in truth" (John 4:21,23,24).

In his answer, Jesus points us away from a geographical location—no holy land. He evidently passes over the building stage of worship and goes straight to the invisible, spiritual, and mental level as he tells the Samaritan woman ". . . the true worshippers shall worship the Father in spirit and in truth." He said the time would come, and yet was "now." It would appear that Jesus is allowing for individuals to determine just where they are on that worship scale. For some, the last stage of worship is now. For others, "the hour cometh." When that time comes for the collective (for the greater percentage), then obviously the brotherhood of followers will not need to be organized.

A mighty movement.

For the laying of her church's cornerstone in 1894, Mary Baker Eddy echoed Jesus' prophecy "But the hour cometh . . . " with a corresponding prophecy of her own, "But the time cometh when the religious element, or Church of Christ, shall exist alone in the affections, and need no organization to express it" (*Miscellaneous Writings* p. 145). A few years earlier she had written, "Material organization is requisite in the beginning; but when it has done its work, the purely Christly method of teaching and preaching must be adopted" (*Miscellaneous Writings*, p. 359).

It is difficult to foresee exactly when and how the changing form of church may make the transition back to the "purely Christly method of teaching and preaching." However, we are able to gain many glimpses right now of what actually constitutes the widespread Church of Christ. There is one unmistakable key feature that will distinguish this Church, and Jesus pointed it out for us, "By this shall all men know that ye are my disciples, if ye have love one to another" (John 13:35).

Mary Baker Eddy spoke of this brotherly love as an "inviolate" bond when she wrote: "The real Christian compact is love for one another. This bond is wholly spiritual and inviolate" (*Miscellaneous Writings* p. 91).

John Greenleaf Whittier likewise described spiritual worship and brotherhood in one of his beautiful poems (often sung as a hymn).

> O, he whom Jesus loved has truly spoken,
> That holier worship, which God deigns to bless,
> Restores the lost, and heals the spirit broken,
> And feeds the widow and the fatherless.
>
> Then brother man, fold to thy heart thy brother,
> For where love dwells, the peace of God is there:
> To worship rightly is to love each other;
> Each smile a hymn, each kindly deed a prayer.
>
> Follow with reverent steps the great example
> Of him whose holy work was doing good;
> So shall the wide earth seem our Father's temple,
> Each loving life a psalm of gratitude.

From the clear descriptions just given, it will not be difficult to recognize the Church of Christ!

While I was working on the last chapter of this book, a man called who had found *The Ultimate Freedom* in prison. Recently released, he was ordering two copies (one in English and one in Spanish) for sharing. He said he was now looking beyond himself and thinking of how he could serve others. At the same time a woman, whose former employment had come to an end when her employer passed on, was helping me with copyediting. She became interested in the concepts expressed in this book and in *The Ultimate Freedom*. In fact, her level of interest was so great, she remarked that she may need to change some of her beliefs. She went on to say that wouldn't be a problem, because she was sincerely seeking the truth.

When the call came from the former inmate, this woman was so impressed she asked me to send him another two copies and to deduct the cost of the extra books from her pay. Here was a man (recently out of prison) and a woman (recently out of work) both hoping, *and paying*, to give inspiration to others.

Jesus' mission was to free all humanity from the prison of sin, sickness and death. He showed us the Christ, the way to God who is Truth and Love. We all must change our beliefs along the way. If we didn't need to, then we would already be there.

As the merely ritual sense of worship yields to the habitual performance of daily deeds, the Church of Christ will become increasingly visible.

Those dedicated to the understanding and demonstration of divine Life and Love are indeed a worldwide society, a mighty movement, or the Church of Christ. With feet firmly planted on the rock of spiritual understanding this will be a healing church. Its members-at-large will warmly embrace that which offers man a full salvation from all mortality—from sin, disease and death. Yes, they will understand Truth—the Science of the Christ—and they will claim their birthright as children of God. Under one Parent their brotherhood will be indisputable evidence of that unity for which Christ Jesus prayed.

A great army of peaceful participants will demonstrate in their own lives what Truth is and does for mankind. With love for God and man, we will be that society, that movement, that church, that army. Our service of compassion will be performed on the holy ground of gratitude everywhere, in every country, every moment of the day, because our divine, scientific Principle is universal and unconfined.

We will also provide our brotherly service in buildings, airports, desert outposts, or campgrounds and we'll allow the form to change so that we, like the Good Samaritan, may come where our brothers and sisters are and not pass by them. Where will they be and how will we meet them? We'll meet them as they are buying medicine in the drugstore. We'll meet them as they ask for money outside the post office. We'll meet them running for a bus. We'll meet them on the El in Chicago. We'll meet them over the telephone or by e-mail. We'll see them in prisons—held by the state or in prisons of grief and sickness.

Yes, we'll meet them and we'll feed them with healing truths. We'll meet them as they sit in cars outside our church buildings or as they sit in police cars on the way to jail. We'll go to them because we will hear their call. And we will hear their call because we are listening to God, the divine Love that meets all human need. And if we've experienced trying times, we will know how much others also need comforting, and we will comfort them with ". . . the comfort wherewith we ourselves are comforted of God" (II Corinthians 1:4).

And when we meet them, we'll approach gently with kindness, patience, and with these words in our hearts, "You are so loved." They'll see it in our smile and feel it in our handshake, for they, too, are on that spiritual journey to eternal Life and divine Love. All mankind must eventually solve the problem of being by understanding Truth, which is God. At that point, there will be no need to ask if we are loved by the Supreme Being, for we will constantly hear the heavenly message, "It's forever that I love you." And if that isn't being at home, I don't know what is!

The twenty-third Psalm is a beautiful description of our journey home. The journey is being shepherded, guided each step of the way as we are led to have rest and refreshment; as we walk through challenging situations and death threats. All of "life's illusions" will be dispelled here and hereafter as we come into the full recognition of spiritual life and of harmony, God's heavenly kingdom right here, right now.

In *Science and Health* the spiritual sense of this psalm is given on page 578, where the word "Lord" is replaced with the incorporeal, spiritual concept of Deity as found in the Gospels. The shepherd for our spiritual journey home is divine Love.

[DIVINE LOVE] is my shepherd; I shall not want.

[LOVE] maketh me to lie down in green pastures: [LOVE] leadeth me beside the still waters.

[LOVE] restoreth my soul [spiritual sense]: [LOVE] leadeth me in the paths of righteousness for His name's sake.

Yea, though I walk through the valley of the shadow of death, I will fear no evil: for [LOVE] is with me; [LOVE'S] rod and [LOVE'S] staff they comfort me.

[LOVE] prepareth a table before me in the presence of mine enemies: [LOVE] anointeth my head with oil; my cup runneth over.

Surely goodness and mercy shall follow me all the days of my life; and I will dwell in the house [the consciousness] of [LOVE] for ever.

The joyful announcement will inevitably be made:

Ignorance, sin, disease, death—all mortality, have left the building! Our conscience and our consciousness are clear.

We are home!

About the author

Auriel Wyndham Livezey resides in Long Beach, California. As a young woman, she entered the full-time practice of spiritual healing in 1968 helping others to find spiritual solutions to every aspect of life. Since 1971, she has also enjoyed giving inspirational talks, whether to a few or to 5,000 people.

A native of Australia, Auriel was academically educated in that country, also in Canada, Europe, and the United States. She has been, and is being, spiritually educated by the study of the *Holy Bible,* aided by Mary Baker Eddy's spiritual discovery set forth in her book *Science and Health with Key to the Scriptures.*

After setting up Mountaintop Publishing in 1994 to publish her dad's book *The Ultimate Freedom,* Auriel subsequently published two books of her own as well as her two musical plays. She has written and produced a number of musical recordings. Details may be found on www.MountaintopPublishing.com.

With great gratitude, Auriel acknowledges her childhood spiritual lessons guided by loving parents, and especially those wonderful learning experiences with her beloved husband Glen. Most of all she gives heartfelt thanks to her heavenly Parent from Whom she has received *Quiet Answers.*

About the illustrator

Hank Richter was born in Cleveland, Ohio, and graduated with honors from the Philadelphia Museum School of Art. After many years of owning a successful advertising agency in Phoenix, Hank's exposure to Western art led him to devote his full time to producing fine art. He is nationally recognized for his painting and sculpture, specializing in Western Art themes.

Though Hank's artwork is included in major private and public art collections, you may also gain ready access to his inspiring work on the website, www.artofthecowboy.com.

The talents of Hank Richter further appear in his cartoons, and in the children's books which he writes and illustrates. Teaching Sculpture and Cartooning classes at The Principia College, Elsah, Illinois, as well as civic and community projects, are part of the productive and fulfilling life that Hank and Janet Richter lead. Their home is in Phoenix, Arizona.